D1534930

Falling In Love
With Life

—■—

A Guide to EFFORTLESS
Happiness and Inner Peace

By

Thomas M. Kelley, Ph.D.

First edition

Breakthrough Press, Rochester, Michigan

Published by:

 Breakthrough Press
P.O. Box 81226
Rochester, Mi. 48308 - 1226

All rights reserved. No part of this book may be reproduced or transmitted in any form or by any means, electronic or mechanical, including photocopying, recording or by any information storage and retrieval system without written permission from the author, except for the inclusion of brief quotations in a review.

© Copyright   1996 by Thomas M. Kelley

First Printing   1997

Publishers Cataloging in Publication Data

Kelley, Thomas M.

  Falling in Love With Life : a guide to effortless happiness
and innerpeace / Thomas M. Kelley. - Rochester Hills, Mi. :
Breakthrough Press, 1997 .
      p. ; cm.
   ISBN : 0-9656511-3-4
    1. Happiness. 2. Mental Health I. Title
BF 575.H27   1997
158.1 - dc21   96-80246

00   99   98   *   5   4   3   2   1

Printed in the United States of America

To My Mother

Contents

Acknowledgments

For over 35 years, I searched for the secret to more enduring peace of mind and lasting happiness. Finally, my search has ended. The breakthrough principles of Psychology of Mind have led me to a level of contentment, vitality, and happiness that I never before thought possible!

Writing this book was a labor of love. I want to acknowledge all the wonderful, caring people who coached me along the way.

To Albert Ellis, Robert Harper, Wayne Dyer, and David Burns, who first helped me see the relationship between thought and my experience of life.

To Werner Erhard and Landmark Education Corporation, whose powerful courses first helped me distinguish the experience of living life in the moment from living life in my memories.

To Rick Suarez, Roger Mills, and Darlene Stewart, whose ground-breaking book, *Sanity, Insanity, and Common Sense*, started me on a journey to a deeper, more profound level of understanding human psychological functioning.

To Joe Bailey, Sandy Krot, Jeff Timm, Gordan Trockman, Keith Blevens, Dicken Bettinger, Carol Ringold, and Rita Shuford, whose words and writings helped me quiet my analytical thinking.

A special thanks to Dr. Roger C. Mills, Co-Founder of Psychology of Mind, for his wise, kind, patient, invaluable coaching, and for his exceedingly generous and inspiring Foreword to this book.

To Judy Sedgeman, for her unrelenting commitment to the integrity of the principles and concepts of this powerful new psychology. Her coaching and compassion moved me to a new level of grounding, and thus, a completely new book.

To Dr. George Pransky, Co-Founder of Psychology of Mind, for his generous guidance and firm commitment that this book be a real contribution to people.

To my friends and colleagues; Daniel Kennedy, Lewis Smith, Al Yezbick, Steven Stack, Luther Gillispie, Randy McClure, Cathy Johnson and Norman Goldner, for their insightful suggestions and enthusiastic support for this project.

To Anne Callahan, for her friendship and impeccable typing.

To my dear, loyal friends; Dan, Shirley, Jan, Wally, Dennis, Rena, Bob, Dorothy, Manolo, Ingrid, Vito, Roseanna, Terry, Donna, Doug, Judy, Lew, Karen and Butch for putting up with my "ego" over the years, and loving me anyway.

To all my clients and students who helped me deepen my level of understanding these breakthrough principles.

I wrote this book especially for the angels in my life; Marty, Kathy, Ricky, Penny, Brenna, and Danny. I'm blessed to have these wonderful, loving people around me. Thank you for your never-ending, unconditional love and support. I love you all.

Foreword

I want to express my gratitude for Tom Kelley's efforts in writing this book. Although Tom is a tenured Professor at Wayne State University and a licensed psychologist, he has never rested on his laurels. He has stayed open and respectful of new ideas. He has not acted as though his accomplishments in the field of psychology privileged him to feel satisfied or to assume he had all the answers. In 1989, he was exposed to the outcomes of several pilot programs conducted in collaboration with residents of inner city communities in Miami. In these communities, Psychology of Mind (POM) had been used as the foundation for resident empowerment and community revitalization efforts. Looking as a researcher at the outcomes of these programs, Tom responded with a refreshing openness and insatiable curiosity. He became committed to understanding why these results were far beyond those achieved from other models of empowerment. He observed leadership, motivation and levels of self esteem in these communities that he could see would benefit people in all walks of life.

Since then he has studiously applied himself to grasping the impact and potential of these discoveries for the field of psychology. Although a respected academic and oft published author of professional journal articles, Tom was not satisfied with just an intellectual understanding of new ideas in the field. He sincerely wanted these discoveries to benefit himself, in terms of his own growth and happiness. He realized very deeply the truth of the admonition, "physician heal thyself" recognizing that he could not help others find deeper levels of mental health unless he himself could see substantive changes in this direction *in his own* psychological functioning. He had the humility and dedication to his field to become a serious student of Psychology of Mind. Over the last several years, while he studiously applied himself to grasping this paradigm, I have come to admire his willingness to question his thinking at every juncture, and to look, from a deeper vantage point, at things that he felt had previously helped him in life.

His journey is documented in this book. In addition to the case studies used to demonstrate the kinds of changes that result from the logic and power of this approach, Tom was willing to share his own examples. His stories of this own life experiences illustrate how these findings about the nature of our moment to moment mental processes can help us all find deeper levels of happiness, and can allow anyone to achieve a wiser, more understanding perspective on life. His willingness to utilize these insights in his life has allowed him to write a self help book that can assist the reader find what Tom has found for himself.

The Case of Change and Human Nature

The findings reported in this text provide fascinating clues to less personal, broader facts about human nature and change. They offer a more generic understanding of how we all tick psychologically. Recognizing these common denominators as factual, as applying across cultures and personality types or life styles, automatically triggers a process of personal evolution and change. This process is one that moves us continually toward increased well being and mature healthy thinking. The discovery of these truths has had the benefit of making the personal growth process more genuine, while less personal, far easier and more invigorating. Applying these principles in our personal lives becomes a delightful journey of discovery, one much different than "working on" ourselves. The tone of delight and enthusiasm of this book reflects Tom's excitement of making this discovery, a realization that has now motivated hundreds of professionals and researchers to explore and understand these findings more fully.

The True Catalyst for Change

Historically, the early focus in psychology was on identifying pathology and on analyzing past traumas. As a consequence, the field of psychology placed more importance on our negative thinking and emotions, on catharsis, on "dealing with" our problems and hang-ups. The discoveries leading to the new Psychology of Mind paradigm have shown us just the opposite. The real power for change lies in the direction of deeper, more natural, more forgiving, more gratifying, more compassionate and loving feelings. These qualities of feelings emerge first for ourselves and then toward others as we recognize that we are all in the same boat. These higher quality, deeper feelings; feelings that stem of our "free flowing," wiser mode of thought, are actually the real catalysts for change. This book points the reader toward both a recognition and unleashing of these qualities of feelings and perceptions.

One of the truths recognized by Tom, reported here in an extremely helpful way, stemmed from his earlier participation in various self help and personal growth movements. He realized that well meaning people had, inadvertently, been looking in a misleading direction to accomplish stress reduction or to create positive change. The focus on people's personal thoughts, emotions and past experiences obscured deeper truths and principles of human nature and human functioning. As Tom points out very clearly in this book, to recognize and benefit from these deeper truths, we must first move away from too much of a focus on our personal thoughts and emotions. Putting these emotions and thoughts in a broader perspective allows change to occur without having to work through all of our past, without having to constantly confront or manipulate our thinking or our current difficulties. We can go directly into a healthier mode of thought that bypasses the qualities of thought and affect that got us in trouble in the first place.

The Gift of Thought

As human beings, we were granted the ability to breath. We have a physical immune system. We have the ability to digest food for energy and other natural health maintenance or health enhancing capacities. We were also given the gift of thought. The explorations leading to the POM paradigm convinced us that the gift of thought is the most powerful capacity of any in our repertoire of inborn faculties as human beings. Understanding how to use this gift in the way it was meant to be used is perhaps the most beneficial outcome anyone could realize from this book.

In our work over the last twenty years, these discoveries have been applied across cultures, across diagnoses and across settings with equally positive outcomes. Our appreciation of the ability of individuals in all walks of life to benefit and change from this understanding was strengthened immensely by the extent of growth in clients of clinical, organizational and community based projects conducted over the last twenty years. The majority of people studied in these programs moved from being largely incapacitated, highly dependent clients to becoming healthy, productive citizens. The scope of these results has been amply documented in demonstration programs from Miami, to the South Bronx, in Hawaii and throughout the mid-west, to Oakland, CA and South Central Los Angeles.

The Depth of the Human Potential

This wide variety of applications has shown, in a compelling way, the true depth and promise of the human potential. I am certainly more thrilled and more respectful than ever as the fruits of this understanding multiply, and continue to get stronger after twenty years. I observe the depth of this potential in everyone because I see it unfolding daily in my work. At times, in this book, what Tom is pointing the reader toward seems almost too idealistic, unachievable or unrealistic. I now know with certainty that, at the very least, we all can achieve a relatively stress free, enjoyable, fruitful and richer life that, at the same time, contributes to the well being of others. This potential, and much more, exists as a very natural state of mental functioning in all of us. It is always responsive when we realize how to tap into it. Once tapped, it continues to unfold naturally throughout our lives in an almost magical way.

In this book, Tom has presented these ideas and findings in a down to earth manner. His writing style is direct, it is easy to understand, and eminently graspable. As a result, the reader can quickly apprehended the import and usefulness of his ideas. He has been successful at expressing himself in a clear, common sense fashion. This book was not intended as an academic treatise or more theoretical exploration of these principles. While it possesses some limitations in this respect, it is true to its purpose. It's purpose is to help people have a nicer, more fulfilling life; to better fulfill their potential as loving, wise and stable human beings. It will, I am sure, greatly assist lay readers find more happiness, vastly reduce stress and live a more rewarding, satisfying and contented life.

Roger C. Mills, Ph.D.
Co-Founder, Psychology of Mind

CAUTION!
Please Read Before Proceeding

Please read this book at your own risk! The breakthrough principles presented here, when clearly understood, may be hazardous or even fatal to your "ego" or "self-image." If you choose to proceed and happen to catch on to these powerful principles, you will be at great risk of unleashing so much **effortless** happiness and inner peace that your "ego" may actually disappear!

You may discover that your urges to "look good," to "be right," and to "prove yourself" are dramatically reduced. You may notice a striking reduction in the level of conflict and struggle in your personal relationships. You may even put the past back in the past, and start living more fully in the present.

Please be forewarned! The "egos" of many people who have read this book have not been able to withstand the natural happiness, self-esteem, and serenity that has been released. May they rest in peace!

Living With the "Mental Flu" and Searching

I used to be "normal." Like most people in this culture, I'd gotten used to living with several chronic symptoms of the mental flu! For years, I did everything that I thought would lead me to lasting happiness and peace of mind. By age 29, I had my Ph.D., an attractive condominium, a shiny red convertible, a pretty girlfriend, money in the bank, a professorship at a major urban research university, and a thriving psychotherapy private practice. Yet, even with all the "right stuff," my moments of happiness and inner peace were fleeting.

Also, I had a great self-image. Actually, most of the time, "it" had me. I prided myself on being attractive, intelligent, serious, articulate, ambitious, and successful. Most of the people who knew me as my "image," thought I had it made. Those who knew me better, however, could see beneath the facade. They saw what I knew was there, but for the life of me couldn't seem to shake...a lot of anxiety, unhappiness, and self-consciousness that followed me around like my own shadow.

These uncomfortable feelings were with me most of the time. Frequently, they focused on my physical appearance, usually my face and hair. I was very compulsive about my hair being in place. I avoided activities like swimming that might mess it up. I did frequent "check myself out" rituals and had favorite mirrors in most of the places I visited. Much of the time, my mood seemed to hinge on how I thought I looked from moment to moment. I despised this lousy habit! No matter what I tried, however, I couldn't seem to break it.

Also, I had a tremendous need to prove myself through my abilities and accomplishments. It seemed like I was always competing with and comparing myself to my close male friends. At one point, I had seven different jobs at the same time! I prided myself on this achievement and wore it like a badge of courage. Nonchalantly, I would brag to my friends about these jobs and imagined that they were quite impressed. Years later, I asked some of them what they really thought. Most said they thought I was a little crazy. They were right.

During those crazy days, I would wake up most mornings with butterflies in my stomach, a lump in my throat, and a nervous cough that would come and go. At parties, I would measure my accomplishments against those of my friends to see if I was still at the top of the pecking order. If I ranked myself less than number one, I felt anxious and depressed and would immediately start thinking up new goals to conquer.

In my relationships, I couldn't seem to make a commitment. I always managed to find some fatal flaw...some terminal imperfection in every woman I dated. I would either focus on changing my partner or start feeling resentful and detached. Eventually, my partner would become frustrated and end the relationship. Then, predictably, I would feel "crushed" and try desperately to get her back. When it was clear that the relationship was over, I would likely be depressed for months.

By the time I was thirty-two, I had been divorced twice and finally decided to try some psychotherapy. My therapist was a brilliant and committed man trained in the traditional psychodynamic approach. I usually felt anxious sitting in his reception room waiting for him to open the door from the hallway leading to his office. Finally, his head would appear around the side of the door. Then he would nod to me with a faint smile. That meant it was my turn.

He was cordial and friendly to a point, but always somewhat formal and aloof. Rarely did he share anything personal except on one occasion. During that session he stated proudly, "You know...I've been doing psychotherapy full time for over ten years, and I just read that the average burnout time for therapists is five years!" Yet, he often looked tired and haggard. Occasionally, he would become so drowsy that he had to fight to keep his eyes from closing. At the time, I saw him as a role model. I wanted to be just like him as a therapist.

During our sessions we focused on my past, childhood, and family relationships. We analyzed my insecure feelings, dreams, divorces, and compulsive habits. Pretty typical stuff for most therapy then, and even now. We did this on a weekly basis for about eighteen months. Most of our sessions were quite serious. Usually I felt some degree of anxiety while we talked. I guess I was afraid that some awful part of me that I'd never seen before was going to sneak out at some point and scare the heck out of me! When our sessions ended I felt many different ways...often confused, at times sad, occasionally relieved. Sometimes I felt inspired, but usually in an agitated or driven way.

Overall, I felt somewhat better after completing therapy, a little less compulsive and perfectionistic, even more self-confident. Yet, I could never clearly understand what occurred during therapy that made this difference. Traditional psychotherapy gave me little recognition about how or why my mental health went up a few notches. It left me confused about how to maintain the healthier functioning I had gained. Also, I still wasn't where I wanted to be. I still didn't have the level of understanding necessary to experience genuine self-esteem, happiness, and peace of mind as a way of life.

During therapy, I began reading scads of self-help books. Most of them were based on the cognitive or rational emotive model of psychological functioning. Basically, the cognitive model challenged the commonly held belief that our feelings and perceptions are caused by other people, external events, and outside circumstances. According to the cognitive perspective, every human feeling and perception is determined by people's beliefs or points of view <u>about</u> the events and circumstances in their lives.

For me, there was something very liberating in this perspective. Subsequently, I spent a great deal of time, as these books suggested, actively uncovering, challenging, and refuting my dysfunctional beliefs and viewpoints. I worked diligently at trying to think more rationally. Also, I began using this approach with my psychotherapy clients.

At the time, this new understanding made a significant difference for me. My typical level of mental health went up several notches. Yet, something still seemed to be missing. For example, when I felt really low, it was often difficult to force myself to think more rationally. During my down times, I didn't feel much like actively challenging my irrational beliefs.

Overall, the thought reconditioning tools of cognitive psychology did help me cope better with life. When I used them, they seemed to help loosen the grip of some of my compulsive and perfectionistic habits. However, I still wasn't spending very much time feeling a sense of ease, contented, peaceful, or genuinely happy and fulfilled. Some important understandings still seemed to be missing.

In the summer of 1977, guess where I was again? You got it...searching in the self-help section of another bookstore. As I scanned the shelves, I spotted an intriguing paperback. It's subject was a controversial group training course that had become very popular during the 1970s. The author had completed this course and the book was his description of the experience. Having heard of this popular seminar and being curious to know more about it, I bought the book.

I'll never forget the feeling of aliveness and excitement as I turned each page. What was so exhilarating was the realization that I had spent much of my life living as a kind of impostor. It occurred to me that I had made up a story about myself and my life that I had misguidedly come to see as real. It dawned on me that I was living much of my life as the main character in a story about my life that I had totally made up! I realized that experiencing my life through this thought-created story prevented me from living life more fully in the present.

I was anxious to deepen this new awareness. When I returned to Detroit I immediately enrolled in the next available course. In those days, these seminars were held in large hotel ballrooms. I can't remember the name of the hotel, but I'll never forget what happened the night before the course began. Within two or three hours after checking in, three large cold sores erupted on my lower lip. This was the first and only time in my life that I've ever had cold sores. You can imagine how this went over for someone who thought that his appearance had to be flawless. That very next morning I was going to be sitting in a brightly lit hotel ballroom with around two hundred people. After a mild panic attack, I rushed to a nearby drugstore and bought the strongest non-prescription cold sore medication I could find. Back in my room, I basted those critters most of the night. The medicine didn't even phase them!

The next morning I invented a way to camouflage all three cold sores with one of those sheer, skin-colored Band-Aids. Fortunately, even I had enough sense to realize that the Band-Aid looked more ridiculous than the blisters. Finally, I self-consciously dragged myself into the training room. Nonchalantly, I tried to cover my mouth with my hand as much as possible, and avoided looking directly at the other people. Hey, I did the best I could! Anyway, as the training proceeded, I became so absorbed in the process that I pretty much forgot about the cold sores and started feeling "normal" again.

At that time, the leaders of this course were extremely confrontive. The sessions were long and arduous. The first session started at exactly 8:30 a.m. on Saturday and lasted until perhaps 3:00 a.m. Sunday morning! The Sunday session was nearly as long. Our leader used a number of different strategies. He lectured incessantly, lead us through several closed-eyed processes, and had intense, one-on-one conversations with various participants. Some of the techniques he used were pretty strange. At one point, for example, we all had to imagine that we were rappelling down the side of a huge strawberry! Initially, many of the participants were confused, bored, even outraged.

By the end of the second weekend, however, amazing transformations seemed to occur for many of the participants. Many trainees appeared to experience a breakthrough in their level of mental health. In fact, several seemed to make more progress in just two weekends than most of my "successful" psychotherapy clients after months or even years of therapy!

For example, a number of participants contacted their parents, siblings, or ex-spouses, and told them they loved them or forgave them for hurting, betraying, or abusing them in the past. Some trainees let go of debilitating grudges they'd been holding onto for five, ten, even twenty or thirty years! Several participants had a genuine change of heart about their marital relationships. Some apologized to their partners for past perpetrations like cheating or lying. Many rekindled intense feelings of love and commitment for their family and friends.

In just two weekends, many of the participants genuinely appeared to have put their pasts back in the past and long-held complaints, habits, problems, grudges and resentments seemed to disappear! I'll always remember calling my mother and sister in Florida after the course. I told them how much I loved and appreciated them with more love and intimacy than I'd ever experienced before.

The rapid and dramatic shifts in health that seemed to occur for me and many of the other trainees led me to question many of the core assumptions I'd been taught about how people work psychologically and how they change. Yet, I had no idea how this course worked. For the life of me, I couldn't figure out the source of the striking bursts of health that I'd observed.

Over the next several years I participated in a series of seminars available to graduates of this course. While I always seemed to get value from these classes, an interesting thing began to happen. I found myself drifting back into some of my old self-defeating, perfectionistic habits and anxious feelings. Not as intense as before, but enough to be annoying and perplexing. I figured that I must have lost something that I'd originally gotten from the course. By participating in additional seminars, I secretly hoped to find it again. Occasionally, those original feelings of satisfaction and aliveness would return. Soon, however, they would fade away once again. To my dismay, there was still something missing. I still didn't have the level of understanding necessary to experience the wonderful feelings of genuine mental health as a way of life!

My Missing Breakthrough

In the spring of 1988, guess where I was again? That's right...in the self-help section of the book department in a discount drugstore in Birmingham, Michigan. I was looking for another self-help book to read on a trip to visit my mother and sister in St. Pete, Florida. Finally, I spotted a title that intrigued me, *Sanity, Insanity, and Common Sense,* by Rick Suarez, Roger Mills, and Darlene Stewart. This groundbreaking book presented some important core ideas that eventually led to the realization of the principles of a revolutionary new psychology called Psychology of Mind, or POM.

I clearly remember the exhilaration I experienced as I read this incredible book. Since then, I've devoured virtually every POM book, tape, and video cassette that I could get my hands on. The deeper I understood these remarkable ideas, the clearer I became that the principles of Psychology of Mind represented a true breakthrough for the field of mental health!

The principles of Psychology of Mind clearly explained every state of mind that I'd ever experienced. They made sense of every emotion I'd ever felt. They clarified how at times I could be stuck in tremendous anger, resentment, or anxiety and how, at other times, I could feel intense compassion, love, and respect for just about everyone.

These simple principles explained every perception and reaction that I'd ever had. They accounted for the times I became defensive, irrational, and emotionally unstable as well as my hopeful, inspired, and creative moments. They made sense of my every behavior, from the most foolish and self-destructive to the most wise and compassionate.

Even the most complex human psychological problems and conditions were explained and resolved by understanding the three principles and core concepts of POM and how they interact! Also, these breakthrough understandings provided compelling evidence that everyone is born with the natural source of effortless healthy psychological functioning. This includes a natural self-esteem, effortless peace of mind, and automatic happiness!

I started using the principles of Psychology of Mind in my therapy practice with magnificent success. Many of my clients began moving from simply getting better at coping with life to living with more ease, contentment, and exhilaration. From these healthier psychological perspectives, they began to access an inherent self-esteem, wisdom, and common sense. From this higher vantage point, they could see for themselves more sensible, even creative solutions to their problems.

Also, I started using these principles in my teaching and research at the University. Almost immediately, I noticed a heightened level of interest, exhilaration, and involvement from my students. Many of my criminal justice students, for example, gained a new understanding and compassion for both juvenile and adult offenders. They started taking the deviant behavior of these people less personally. They began to see more effective and common sense ways of treating them within the criminal justice system.

I began writing journal articles applying these new understandings to the problems of at-risk youth, delinquency, adult criminality, and domestic violence. My sense of hope and vision for ending these and other social problems began to expand exponentially.

Psychology of Mind provided me with my missing breakthrough! It led me to a new level of understanding human psychological functioning that completely obliterated what was left of any confusion and struggle. It helped me realize how I learned to be "normal." It empowered me to see how I was taught to short-circuit the natural source of my birthright of effortless, healthy psychological functioning. More importantly, it did so in a gentle, compassionate way that was a joy to experience. No confrontation, no gimmicks, no New Age milarky, no emphasis on struggle or willpower to change. Just quiet, yet profound shifts in understanding.

Through understanding the principles of Psychology of Mind, I have realized my natural human capacity for effortless mental health. These remarkable understandings empowered me to release this natural health as a way of life. They showed me how to quietly rekindle the spontaneous self-expression, satisfaction, well-being, inspiration, enjoyment, and profound happiness that I typically experienced as a child. How can I be so sure about this? I haven't taken a self-improvement course or visited the self-help section of a bookstore <u>to get better</u> since! How good can you stand it!

Chapter 1

Realizing Your Birthright of Effortless Mental Health

Please let me be straight with you right from the start. What's in store for you here isn't another gimmick, short term fix, or empty promise. I know that many of you have read other self-help psychology books. Heaven knows I did, I used to be a self-help book junkie. I read mountains of them. Don't get me wrong, some of them did seem to work. I learned scores of tools and techniques that helped me cope with my typically stressful life. Yet, no matter how many books I read, something always seemed to be missing or left out. Some key pieces to the puzzle of genuine happiness just weren't there. These missing links of understanding kept me from reaching the happiness and peace of mind that I craved.

This book is about those missing pieces. Once I discovered them, I experienced a profound shift in perspective. Suddenly, everything fell into place. Immediately, I realized at a very deep level the existence of our human birthright of natural mental health. Instantly, I recognized how to access the one and only true source of effortless happiness and inner peace.

Through these breakthroughs in understanding, my typical experience of life was transformed. The level of stress, worry, and anxiety in my life has fallen dramatically. I seldom get angry or disappointed anymore. I experience most moments of my life in a more satisfying, fulfilling way. Frequently, I have profound feelings of gratitude and appreciation just for being alive. At last, I can say, without flinching or feeling conflicted, "I feel genuinely happy and satisfied most of the time!" Finally, I can honestly declare, "I've fallen in love with life!"

That's why I waited until now to write this book. I've started writing self-help books on and off for the last twenty-five years. God knows I read enough of them. I certainly kept up with the current jargon and buzz words. Yet, I could never seem to finish one. Why? Probably because I couldn't honestly say that I was genuinely happy most of the time. That awareness, deep in my soul, stopped me from completing a book. How could I coach other people about true happiness if I wasn't that happy? It just didn't seem right.

Also, since there were some important shifts in understanding missing for me, my unfinished books weren't really an expression of my own creativity, wisdom, or full self-expression. Instead, they were mostly reformulations of other people's work. Thus, my enthusiasm and exhilaration while writing them was pretty low.

Believe me, I've been on the search just like many of you. I've read the books, listened to the tapes, done the seminars, and attended the motivational sessions. Later, more often than not, I felt the letdown, confusion, and disappointment. I've even been conned a few times!

Now, however, things are different. Now, I can honestly tell you that I know what's possible for human beings in the arena of happiness and inner peace. More importantly, I've finally discovered the only true way to get there. A way with no gimmicks, no false promises, no empty tunnels, no rugs pulled out from under you. If you're willing to read on with a quiet mind, you'll discover, for yourself, the only way back to your birthright of effortless well-being, self-esteem, peace of mind, and natural happiness!

The Innocent Failure of the Field

The field of psychology has produced hundreds of theories and thousands of studies in its attempt to explain human behavior. By now, you would think that all of this research would have led to a breakthrough in the quality of our mental health. If the field of psychology was on the right track, shouldn't we be experiencing more peace of mind and genuine happiness today than ever before?

Yet, when you look closely at the evidence, it just isn't so. People are physically healthier today and live much longer. Most of us live more comfortably and conveniently today than did our ancestors. Yet, it's virtually impossible to make the case that people today are significantly happier than in generations past. In fact, there's considerable evidence to suggest that human beings are less happy and content today than ever before.

Take work-related stress, for example. Experts estimate the cost of such stress, like lost productivity, medical expenses, and absenteeism, at over 200 billion dollars a year! Add to that our fifty to sixty percent divorce rate, spiraling violent crime, family violence, teen drug use and pregnancy, suicide, school drop-out rates, psychosomatic diseases, violence in the media, racism, sexism, work place violence, job dissatisfaction, family dysfunction, alcoholism, sexual problems, anxiety and depressive disorders, and on and on. Phew! I don't mean to bring you down, but the evidence for lower levels of mental health today just doesn't seem to end.

Even our mental health professionals often suffer from chronic unhealthy moods and high stress. My friend, Joe Bailey, a nationally known addictions counselor, reports that in his field, the average counselor burns out within five years. Treatment counselors last an average of 2.3 years in each job. When Joe asks them why they quit they often say, "The job was just too stressful. I had to get out or crack up!"

What's going on here? What's wrong with this picture? It almost appears that the findings of the experts on human psychological functioning have guided us toward poorer rather than better mental health. What's happening here? Why would such a large group of committed mental health professionals want to lower the level of our psychological functioning? Well, I don't think it's been intentional. It looks to me like the field of psychology has done the best job it could considering its present level of understanding. Unfortunately, the field has innocently missed some important distinctions that have prevented it from making the profound difference it wants to make in the quality of our mental health.

Other scholarly fields have experienced similar barriers as they evolved. Not long ago, for example, geographers thought that the world was flat. Astronomers believed that the sun and planets revolved around the earth. Physicians were convinced that diseases were caused by bad blood. At the time, each field did the best it could with its current understandings, ideas, and theories. When new knowledge was uncovered that better explained a field's observations, that field would experience what's called a breakthrough. It would move to a new level of understanding from which its old beliefs and ideas would eventually be seen as archaic, even ridiculous.

Before such breakthroughs occurred, however, most ordinary people functioned as if the old understandings were gospel. For example, people actually believed that the world was flat. Thus, they wouldn't sail too far from shore, fearing they would fall off the edge. People really thought the earth was the center of the universe and followed faulty calendars based on that belief. People were genuinely convinced that bad blood caused disease. Therefore, they submitted to gruesome medical treatments, like being bled by leeches, which today sound preposterous and barbaric!

Please consider the possibility that a similar dilemma has existed for the field of psychology. What if the field is genuinely committed to improving our mental health, but its present level of understanding can't lead to a breakthrough? However well-intentioned the experts may be, if their understanding is limited, inaccurate, or downright false, the typical level of our mental health won't leap forward.

If our psychological functioning today is generally low, then either the experts are missing some important recognitions, or they've got it right and the rest of us just haven't caught on. I support the first scenario. Some important distinctions have been missing for the field of psychology. Lacking these essential understandings, the field can't break through to a new, more profound level of effectiveness.

If the so-called experts don't accurately understand how we work psychologically, then most of us are in for a more bumpy and less satisfying journey through life. Without accurately understanding our own psychological functioning, many of us are going to spend big chunks of our lives lost in a maze of confusing and contradictory beliefs, misconceptions, and superstitious ideas about who we really are and the way we really work. One frustrating result of this understanding gap is that in our search for more lasting happiness, we're likely to go down many empty tunnels. While each tunnel may appear to be a promising route to genuine happiness, it often leads us further away from the very thing that we're seeking. Thus, lacking a clear understanding of the true source of healthy mental functioning, the field of psychology has inadvertently been making us worse rather than better!

At Last...The Breakthrough Has Happened

Now here's some great news. The one and only true source of effortless contentment, automatic peace of mind, and natural happiness has finally been discovered! The transformational understandings needed to unleash a mental health breakthrough have finally arrived! They're available now in the form of a revolutionary new psychology called Psychology of Mind, or POM.

The simple, yet unprecedented, principles of Psychology of Mind explain human behavior in all of its many forms and variations. They explain why people get upset, why some people are frightened by things that don't frighten others, why negative past events plague people in the present, why it's hard for people to accept change, why people react differently to the same things, why life seems horribly painful sometimes and absolutely wonderful at others times, why happiness seems to occur at random for people, why seemingly "sane" people "go crazy," why some people get over things and truly change their lives, while others stay stuck in cycles of stress and distress.

The three principles of Psychology of Mind explain every state of mind that you've ever experienced. They make sense of every emotion and feeling that you've ever had. They make understandable every one of your reactions and every behavior you've ever done. These simple principles provide the answers to mankind's deepest questions about the mysteries of human life. Even the most complex human psychological problems and conditions can be explained and resolved by understanding the three principles and core concepts of POM and how they interact!

In a nutshell, the key to all the wondrous experiences of effortless, healthy psychological functioning is a shift in understanding about how all human beings experience life. The way back to your birthright of natural, effortless mental health is a breakthrough in understanding about how you work psychologically through your amazing gift of thought.

Now please be crystal clear about what I'm saying here. Please don't let your memories convince you that this is simply another version of something you already know. Let me be absolutely clear. I'm not talking about positive thinking or affirmations. I'm not referring to rational thinking or challenging your dysfunctional thoughts. I'm not speaking about guided imagery, cognitive restructuring, or any other tools or techniques of thought reconditioning.

What I am saying is this. When you experience a shift in understanding about how you work psychologically through your incredible gift of thought, you will automatically and effortlessly move to a healthier level of mental functioning. A breakthrough in understanding is all that it takes. Better yet...it can happen in an instant.

Rediscovering Your Birthright of Natural Mental Health

Again, the key to experiencing healthier levels of psychological functioning lies solely in a vertical leap in understanding. Please trust me...achieving more enduring mental health doesn't take willpower or effort. It doesn't require adversity, struggle, or pain. You don't have to go through mountains of negativity, frightening feelings, or bad memories to get to it. You don't have to struggle to change your thoughts. You don't need to get in touch with any "inner child." You don't have to wade through your past. Forget about confronting or suing your step-parent for abusing you as a child. It isn't necessary to attend daily self-help support groups. You don't have to build up your "self-image." You certainly don't have to scream or have a catharsis!

All you have to do to experience more of your natural mental health is have a profound shift in understanding exactly how you work psychologically. You have to recognize, for yourself, exactly what allows your birthright of effortless, healthy psychological functioning to spring to life. You have to realize the natural, healthy way that your precious gift of thought was designed to work. Also, it's helpful to see how you innocently learned to abuse one of your thinking abilities and short-circuit the healthy operation of your wondrous gift of thought.

From this new level of understanding, you'll be empowered to access the only true source of healthy psychological functioning. From your new level of understanding, you'll realize how to unleash more of the effortless peace of mind and genuine happiness that you were meant to experience most of the time. You may even find yourself falling in love with the life of your dreams!

Please let me share two analogies to clarify what I mean by a shift in understanding. First, imagine that you've taken the same route to work for the past ten years and truly believed it to be the very best way. What if someone showed you another way that, when you looked with an open mind, you realized was not only a faster way, but a safer and more scenic one as well. Would it take a lot of effort or struggle to switch to this new way? Would you stick to your old route just to be right or to avoid looking foolish for taking the old way for so long? Probably not. If you could see clearly, for yourself, that the new way was truly better, safer, and more scenic than the old one, you'd likely start using it immediately. Oh, you might feel a little sheepish for not seeing the new way sooner, but this feeling would quickly pass and you'd just be happy as a clam with the better way!

Try one more analogy. Imagine that your journey through life is like driving an automobile. Pretend that you, and most everyone else for that matter, were taught to steer your life vehicle by turning the rear view mirror instead of the steering wheel. Imagine that just about everyone had been taught to steer through life in this misguided way. Can you see how this mis-education about steering would drastically impede your ability to drive in the direction of your desired feelings, behaviors, and goals? For example, you'd think you were steering in the right direction and then, suddenly, you'd crash. Every now and then you might reach your desired destination, but only when life's road happened to match the direction of your steering. More often than not, however, after steering very carefully with the rear view mirror, the rug would be pulled out from under you. You'd seldom reach any truly satisfying or fulfilling place.

Can you imagine what might happen after several months or years of steering through life like this? You might start driving slowly and cautiously to lengthen the time between collisions. You might give up altogether, and look for someone else to drive for you. You might decide that crashing was good and added something to your character. Perhaps you'd join a self-help support group for poor steerers. You might stop driving completely, and just work at decorating your vehicle. You might create an imaginary road in your mind that turned in sync with your steering. Or, you might just floor it and take your chances!

Through the breakthroughs in understanding waiting for you on our journey, you'll instantly discover a fast, safe, and scenic route to more lasting happiness. You'll be empowered to put your hands on the steering wheel of healthy psychological functioning. When you do, you'll instantly, peacefully, and effortlessly find yourself cruising in the neighborhood of genuine mental health.

Imagine what your life would be like if you could clearly see the road to high quality psychological functioning and had the steering realizations needed to get there. Well, buckle up, because that's exactly where we're heading. How good can you stand it!

Chapter 2

Understanding and Listening for Breakthroughs

I t's time to get moving toward some breakthroughs. Please remember, the purpose of our journey together is for you to experience some profound new realizations about your psychological functioning. Through these powerful shifts in understanding, more of your natural happiness and inner peace will be effortlessly and automatically released!

I'd like to suggest that we start with some coaching about the true nature of breakthroughs. Why? Because the better you understand breakthroughs, the more you can maximize the conditions that allow them to occur.

One interesting thing about breakthroughs in understanding is that they simply can't happen if you're deliberately looking for them through what you already know. In other words, it's virtually impossible to have a breakthrough when you're actively using your intellect or analytical thinking to compare, judge, agree with, or evaluate the principles and concepts that I'm going to share with you. A shift in understanding can't occur while you're deliberately processing these new distinctions through your already-existing memories about yourself, the nature of change, personal growth, or how to be happy.

With your permission, therefore, I'd like to make this request. For the time being, please forget about everything you've ever learned about human psychological functioning. While you're reading this book, please put on the back burner all of the knowledge you've accumulated about yourself, your personality, your past, your self-image...anything psychological. Remember, if what you already knew held the answer to effortless happiness and inner peace, you probably wouldn't be reading this.

Another important quality of breakthroughs is that they happen instantly. Suddenly, a shift in understanding will occur for you, seemingly from out of the blue. Like an "ah hah," breakthroughs show up spontaneously. Being willing to have one is very helpful. Being relaxed, at ease, with a quiet, clear mind is even better. Why? Because it's impossible to deliberately will a breakthrough to happen or to try and make one happen. Trying, like listening through what you already know, actually short-circuits the natural source of breakthroughs. You'll be much more likely to experience a sudden shift in understanding if you lighten up, clear your mind, and trust that it will happen.

Next, breakthroughs are typically accompanied by enlivening feelings like exhilaration and inspiration. Instantly, you'll experience this incredible shift in understanding. Without any change in the content of your life, you'll experience a transformation or sudden shift in context or the way you relate to or perceive your life. This experience is often exhilarating. It can take your breath away. Why? Because instantly, you'll see new possibilities for living that you've never seen before. The "stuff" in your life will remain exactly the same, but your perspective will be altered, often in an incredibly powerful way!

Another important quality of breakthroughs is that they're permanent.   Once you've experienced a breakthrough in understanding, you'll never forget or lose it. Occasionally, its clarity may fade to some extent. In a lower mood, for example, you might find yourself temporarily drifting back into your old perspective. However, when you're in a state of mind to see it again, it will reappear as fully and clearly as ever. Once you've had an understanding breakthrough, it's always available to you.

Here's an example of a breakthrough that I know most of you have already experienced. Please think back for a moment to when you were a child...say about five or six years old. Can you remember the experience of riding a two-wheel bicycle for the very first time? Riding a "two-wheeler" required that you experience a shift in understanding about the physical principle of "balance."

Now, before attempting to ride, you could have gone to your local library and studied for months about the nature of balance. Unfortunately, all the technical information in the world wouldn't have made much difference. In fact, trying to remember all the facts you learned about balance would likely have delayed your breakthrough. Why? Because balance is an understanding shift you just had to "get."

For me it happened like this. First, I grabbed the handlebars and pushed my bike forward to gain some momentum. Next, I put my feet on the pedals and pushed down on them as hard as I could. Then, I fell several times, skinning both knees in the process. I kept doing this over and over again until finally I experienced this sudden breakthrough with balance. Instantly, I was riding!

If you recall, this experience was pretty sensational. "I'm riding, I'm riding. Mom! Dad! Look! Watch me. I'm riding!" Instantly, you saw a slew of new possibilities unleashed by this breakthrough...freedom, independence, new places to go, new people to meet, time saved, and on and on!

Of course, your breakthrough with balance was permanent. If you didn't ride again for fifty years and were physically capable, you could find a bike and go. You might be a little rusty at first, but your transformed relationship with balance would return to you very quickly.

Here's a final truth about breakthroughs. Unfortunately, you can't coach people to have a breakthrough through some fixed recipe or formula. I wish you could, but you can't. I could have experts talk to you for hours about the experience of balance, or what having a baby is like, or what swimming feels like, or what being "in the zone" is like for an athlete. I could have Nobel prize winners lecture to you about all of these things. They could point to them using words, charts, and diagrams. They could dance around them with you. No matter what they did, however, they couldn't get you to experience any of these things on cue. People have such experiences when they have them. You'll have a breakthrough in understanding when you do, and not one second sooner!

Breakthrough Listening

Perhaps the best way to maximize your chances of experiencing a breakthrough in understanding has to do with your listening. If you're willing to listen to what's coming in a particular way, you'll dramatically increase your likelihood of having a profound shift in understanding. If you're willing to listen in this powerful way, your chances of being hit on the noggin by a breakthrough will increase substantially.

First, it's very helpful to listen with humility. This means listening from outside the confines of your memories, or what you already know. Some people call it, "listening for not knowing." All this means is that you try your best not to deliberately fit what's coming into the stuff you already know. Why? Because by listening for not knowing, you free up the source of your natural intuition and common sense to effortlessly listen for you. It's this natural listening ability that precedes your memories that has the vision to spot a breakthrough.

It's much better to quietly reflect on, rather than deliberately try to understand, the distinctions that we'll visit. Believe me, this isn't just more, better, or different psychological information, tips, or techniques. This is about the one and only true source of effortless and automatic mental health. Psychology of Mind is a revolutionary paradigm. When you experience it, for yourself, more of your natural happiness and peace of mind will instantly be released!

In this culture, most of us have learned to listen primarily in a very low quality way. Most of us listen while we're deliberately using our intellect to compare, analyze, and judge every bit of new information. Most of us don't realize that this artificial health-robbing listening habit short-circuits the natural source of our innate wisdom and creative intelligence. Thus, it's very helpful to relax and quiet this effortful, breakthrough-blocking listening habit. Again, please remember, if what you already knew held the true answer to enduring happiness, it's likely that you wouldn't be reading this.

Please try and listen with humility and a quiet, clear mind. Check your "ego" at the door. Listen with the curiosity and innocence of a healthy child. Calm your intellect or analytical thinking. Set aside your judging and evaluating. Allow the ideas that we'll explore to resonate with your natural intuition and common sense.

Please try on the coming distinctions as if you were shopping for some new clothes. See how they fit. See if they click for you. Your natural wisdom will automatically guide you if you're willing to suspend your loud analytical listening. I guarantee that when you have your first breakthrough in understanding, you'll be thrilled that you listened for <u>not</u> knowing. Try it and see. You've got nothing to lose but stress and unhappiness!

A Very Peaceful Journey

Now that you know how to listen for breakthroughs, let me quiet any apprehension or anxiety you may be feeling. Our journey together will be very peaceful and serene. I know that some of you are presently, or have been in counseling or therapy. If not, most of you have opinions about this process. You probably know that many forms of counseling are based on the belief that you have to get worse before you can get better...that you've got to focus on and analyze painful past events, dredge up and re-experience early childhood traumas and re-live painful memories from the past. In other words, no pain...no gain!

I'd like to suggest that these ideas are misguided, even archaic. Please trust me...you don't have to go through negativity to get healthy! This would be like having a headache, going to the doctor, and having the doctor tell you that you need a little stomach flu to cure the headache. This would be absurd, and so is the superstition about getting better through negativity and pain misguidedly held by so many well-intentioned therapists.

The famous anthropologist, Ashley Montagu, once said, "Psychoanalysis is the study of the id by the odd!" Well, that's not where we're heading on this expedition. First of all, this isn't therapy, this is coaching. I'm requesting your permission to coach you about the absolute principles or facts of human psychological functioning...to teach you how to regularly access the one and only true source of effortless happiness and inner peace.

While being coached, however, there is one slightly uncomfortable feeling that would be helpful for you to experience. This is the feeling of foolishness. Why? Because from the new level of understanding you're going to access, you'll realize that your old perspective had you do some pretty foolish things. When people first had the astounding realization that the world was round, it also occurred to them that being afraid of falling off the edge was pretty silly. On our journey, however, feeling sheepish is a good sign. Here, feeling foolish means that you're catching on, having breakthroughs, and seeing new possibilities for the future. So please relax, lighten up, and quiet your mind. Listen carefully for not knowing. Feel sheepish as often as possible, and get ready to fall in love with life. How good can you stand it!

Chapter 3

It's Time to Stop Searching: Understanding Who You **Really** Are

I used to be a searcher. From the college semester I took my first psychology course, I was always trying to find myself. I became a regular visitor to the self-help psychology shelves in several local bookstores. I bought loads of self-improvement tapes. I listened to countless motivational speakers, spiritual gurus, and radio-talk shrinks. I attended scads of psychological training courses, seminars, and workshops. I completed scores of counseling and psychotherapy sessions. I was on what seemed to be a never-ending expedition to discover my true or authentic identity.

Helping people understand themselves and discover "who they really are" is a billion dollar industry in this culture. Bookstores and libraries are overflowing with self-help books, manuals, tapes, and videos designed to help people "find themselves." The self-help movement in this country has produced thousands of support groups. These well-intentioned groups help people unravel their past so they can "get in touch with themselves" and overcome all kinds of bad habits and addictions. Motivational speakers, self-help books, tapes, and self-improvement courses abound, all designed to help people discover their "true self" or "real identity." Yet, even with all these well-intentioned volumes, courses, support groups, and gurus, people today seem to be searching more than ever for "who they really are!"

How often have you or someone you know said things like, "I seem to have lost myself lately," "I just don't know who I am anymore," or "I know I'll find my true self one day if I just keep searching." Many people seem to move in and out of a firm sense of personal identity. One minute they think they know who they really are...the next minute they're not so sure. Some days we seem to be "in touch with ourselves." Other days we feel more like impostors.

Often, people's experience of "self" or "identity" seems to be elusive, in a state of flux, or even a downright mystery. Therefore, the first breakthrough in understanding that would be helpful to experience concerns the true nature of "self" or "identity." Why? Because when you're unclear about the exact nature of your true self, it's much more likely that you'll spend a lot of time being out of sync with life as it comes at you point blank in each moment. Like a piano out of tune or a movie out of focus, your experience of life is often going to be fuzzy and discordant to the degree that you're confused about or still searching for your "true self."

Unfortunately, we live in a culture that teaches us a lot of misinformation about who we really are. Beginning at birth, many of us were taught that both our identity and self-worth were tied to a slew of external conditions and circumstances. For example, many people have learned that their worth and identity are attached to their achievements or accomplishments. When these people produce the results and outcomes they want, they tend to feel secure and worthwhile. On the other hand, when they fail at something, or get passed by for a promotion, the same people can lose their bearings and start doubting themselves. Some may even panic and have a full-blown identity crisis!

Other people have inadvertently learned that their identity is tied to their emotions. These people think that the particular emotions they experience in some way define who they are. For example, people who typically feel other people's pain may think of themselves as sensitive or high-strung individuals. Others, quick to anger, may see themselves as volatile, hot-tempered or aggressive people. Individuals who seldom have certain feelings like empathy or compassion may come to view themselves as cold and uncaring. Others, good at worrying and feeling anxious, may see themselves as heroic providers of an early warning danger service, like sailors looking out for icebergs from the crow's nest of a ship.

Many people have been taught that who they are is their opinions, beliefs, and points of view. For these individuals, their sense of worth and identity revolves around proving that they're "right." When the opinions and viewpoints of such people are challenged, they tend to feel challenged, as if they actually were these points of view.

Finally, many people have learned that their "true identity" is somehow linked to their personality. These people think that who they are is some combination of fixed personality traits...some of these traits, not much of these, a lot of those, and perhaps none of these. Some people can virtually become paralyzed if life calls for a personality trait that they don't think they have. Say that a bold or assertive action would make perfect sense at a particular moment in time. If a person sees only "shy" on their personality menu, then "shy" tends to show up. Ask that person why and it's likely he'll say, "That's just me...I'm a shy person."

Why is it so hard for all these searching people to find or discover their "true identity?" A major reason for this predicament is that by the time people start deliberately thinking about "who they really are," they've already lost touch with the high quality experience of living where "identity" and "self" aren't important...where in fact, they don't even exist! By the time people begin searching for their "true identity," they're already thinking primarily in a way that won't let them experience it. Put another way, the very condition that has people experience a need or urge to "find themselves," inadvertently causes them to move further and further away from the experience of who they really are. Paradoxically, the more people try to find themselves, the more confused and disillusioned they tend to become!

Who You Really Aren't

With your permission, I'd like to propose something that may surprise or even startle some of you. I'd like to suggest something that may allow you to stop, once and for all, your futile search to find your "true self." You won't have to read anymore self-help books, listen to anymore tapes, take anymore courses, attend anymore motivational sessions, at least not for the purpose of discovering who you really are.

I'd like to begin by exposing a few "artificial identities" that I know you're really not. It's likely that many of you may still think that you are one or more of these false identities. Perhaps your parents, teachers, friends, even a therapist have told you that you are one or more of the following. Please trust me...you're not.

Here goes. You're not your emotions. You experience emotions...but they're not who you are. You're not your beliefs, opinions, ideas, or points of view. They're all simply chains of thought that you've learned along the way...they're not who you are. You're not your accomplishments. Achievements are the things you've done in life...they're not your identity. You're not any of your personality traits. You learned them all, likely with some help from your genes, rehearsed them for years, and may have come to mistake them for the real you. Trust me...they're not! You're not the roles you play in the game of life like mother, husband, teacher, or boss. When you were born, roles were already here like pieces on the cultural game board. Some picked you, you picked some others and started playing them...but, they're not who you are. Last but not least, you're not your "self-concept" or your "ego." Both are thought-created "artificial identities." They're certainly not who you really are.

It might be helpful at this point to take a deep breath, relax, and clear your mind. Why? Because now I'd like to ask you to try on an entirely new perspective about your "true self." Now that you know some of the false identities that I've asserted you really aren't, I request that you consider a very different possibility.

To make this perspective easier for you to see, please think back again to your childhood. Try to remember when your parents told you about Santa Claus, the tooth fairy, the Easter Bunny, or some other similar characters if you grew up in another culture. Can you remember how your parents described the eight reindeer flying Santa around on Christmas Eve, the big bunny rabbit hiding colored eggs on Easter morning, and the tooth fairy collecting your bicuspids and leaving money under your pillow in the middle of the night?

As a child, you likely believed that each of these figures was real. You probably didn't realize that all of these characters were mythical figures made up in cultural lore. No...it's likely that you bought into these wonderful stories. As a child, you thought that each of these imaginary characters actually existed. You probably even identified with them. For you, each one came alive as an actual, meaningful figure in your life. Your actions likely mirrored your thoughts about these characters. You probably left milk and cookies out for Santa, your teeth under your pillow for the tooth fairy, and perhaps some carrots for the Easter Bunny and Rudolph.

Please try to remember what it was like for you when you finally realized that these wonderful characters were fictitious. Can you recall how you felt when it finally occurred to you that they were all just illusions...make-believe myths or fairy tales? How did you feel when you first discovered there was no real Santa Claus, or Easter Bunny, or tooth fairy? How did you feel when you learned that it was all a joke? Perhaps a little sad, disappointed...even shocked?

Well, please get ready for another reality check. I'll try to make this one as easy for you to handle as possible. I'm sorry to have to tell you this, but somebody's got to do it. Ready? Here we go. There is no Santa Claus...and you don't have a "true self" out there somewhere waiting to be discovered...please stop searching! There is no tooth fairy...and you don't have a "real identity" inside of you somewhere waiting to be found...please stop looking! There is no Easter Bunny...and you don't have a "self-image" that needs strengthening...please stop working on yourself. Reindeer don't fly...and you aren't some group of "fixed personality traits"...please stop acting like you are!

The bottom line is this. Self, identity, self-image, self-concept, ego, and fixed personality traits don't exist like actual things or entities. If we opened you up and looked around inside, we'd find lots of organs and tissue, but absolutely none of these items. Why? Because each of them is an illusion that exists only in thought. Just like Santa and the Easter Bunny, you may have innocently learned to see these thought-created "identity illusions" as real or true. Just like Rudolph and the tooth fairy, it's likely that you began to identify with some of them. You probably started relating to these illusions as if they were actual things...as if they really existed. Well, I'm suggesting that none of them is real or true. I'm proposing that you can never find them, align yourself with them, strengthen them, or become them. I'm absolutely certain that none of them is who you really are.

Each of these identity myths was made up, invented, created by some well-intentioned psychologists who were trying their best to understand human psychological functioning. These well-intentioned scholars formulated these ideas or concepts in their honest attempt to explain human behavior. Unfortunately, they were off the mark, didn't realize it at the time, and started promoting these thought-created identity superstitions, innocently thinking that they were the truth.

Over time, most people started believing in these "artificial identities," and guess what? When people believe something, their beliefs take form and appear real to them. When people think something is true, they start seeing evidence to validate their view. When you believed in Santa Claus and fairies, for example, didn't these mythical characters look real to you? When people believed that the earth was flat, it really looked flat to them. No kidding! The exact same illusory process has probably occurred for you with each of your believed identities. Perhaps they've come to look absolutely real to you. In fact, all they really are is thought!

It's very helpful to see that self, identity, ego, self-concept, and fixed personality traits aren't real things or entities. It's empowering to fully comprehend that each of these thought-created "identity illusions" is no more true, or real, or right, or accurate than the illusions of the tooth fairy, leprechauns, Santa Claus, unicorns, and the Easter Bunny. They may be fascinating illusions, but that's absolutely all that they are. As such, you can search forever and you'll never find them, have them, align with them, strengthen them, or become them. Impossible...all they are is your thoughts in action!

Perhaps you have a few questions at this point. For example, you might be wondering, "If I'm not a self, an identity, an ego, a self-concept, or a fixed personality, just who or what am I? If I don't have a true self, an authentic identity, an ego, a self-concept, or some fixed personality traits like actual things or entities, then just who or what am I that accounts for my experience of life? If I stop searching for my "true self" - like a thing out there...if I quit trying to build up my ego and self-concept...if I stop thinking of myself as a fixed personality...what would my experience of living be like? Who would I be? How would I feel? How would I see things? What would I do?"

These are all great questions! Trust me, all the answers will appear to you as we proceed together on our journey toward shifts in understanding. The more clearly you see these answers, for yourself, the more thrilled you're going to be with the news you've just received that you're not any of these "identity illusions." Please wait and see.

Who You Really Are

Let's begin by inquiring into the big issue of "who you really are." Before I suggest an answer for you to consider, I'd like to take a little time to prepare you to hear it. Why? Because it's likely that you've never before thought of yourself in the way I'm going to suggest. Thus, when you first hear the answer I'm going to propose, it may sound a little strange or confusing. If you happen to have this reaction, please remember your intention of having a breakthrough in understanding. Please recall how helpful it is to listen quietly and not deliberately analyze something new if you're in the market for a breakthrough. When you first discovered that there wasn't a real Santa Claus, you may have resisted this news with all your might. When people first contemplated the world being round, it probably seemed very strange, if not incredible, to them. I request that you treat this new possibility about "who you really are" like you would a brand new pair of shoes. Take some time to break it in. Keep listening for <u>not</u> knowing. Please consider it with a calm, clear mind and decide for yourself instead of being decided by your artificial identity illusions.

I'd like to ask you to consider the following simple answer to the question of who you really are. Remember, please break it in slowly. Ready...here goes. **Who you really are is a human being with the divine gift of thought. Who you truly are is a human being with the natural ability to think**!

Please let me explain. As a human being, you were born with the precious gift of thought. You didn't come down the chute being a self, an identity, an ego, a self-concept, a fixed personality...or any other such thought-created identity illusion. Very simply, you, like me, were born a human being with the wondrous gift of thought.

That's not all, however. There's a second part to your true identity that's even more magnificent. You were also born with a built-in, natural design for your miraculous gift of thought to function automatically in a healthy way. You were born with an inherent design to think primarily in a way that automatically and effortlessly produces the experience of genuine mental health.

Let me be crystal clear about the answer I'm proposing to the question of who you really are. Again, the answer I'm suggesting is this. **Who you really are is a human being with the divine gift of thought designed to operate naturally in a health-producing way with absolutely no effort from you!**

When your divine gift of thought is operating according to its natural design principles, it automatically and effortlessly produces healthy psychological functioning. Let me be absolutely clear. Below is a list of high quality psychological experiences. When your divine gift of thought is functioning in its natural, effortless, healthy way, you will automatically show up somewhere in the neighborhood of these experiences. Please read each one slowly. Each is a natural, high quality psychological experience that automatically and effortlessly occurs when your divine gift of thought is working in its inherent, natural way:

A calm, peaceful mind

Free-flowing, effortless thinking

Stress-free productivity

Ability to focus and concentrate without effort

Experiencing life as an interesting adventure

Motivated by curiosity and inspiration

More fully present in each moment

Feeling content, satisfied, and fulfilled

Heightened sense of humor

Relaxed, at ease, easy to be with

High capacity for insight and creativity

Focus is on the beauty in life

Happy with the way things are

Common sense, appropriate behavior

Kindness, joy, generosity

Focus on enjoyment, light-hearted

Empathy, compassion, understanding

Cooperation, flexibility, open-minded

Optimistic, positive attitude

Learning from mistakes and moving on

Love, gratitude, and intimacy

In love with life

That's right...I'm suggesting that who you truly are is a human being with the incredible ability to think in a natural, health-producing way with absolutely no conscious effort from you. When our marvelous gift of thought is operating in this natural way, it automatically moves us into healthy psychological functioning. When our divine gift of thought is working in the quiet, effortless way it was designed to work, we automatically feel balanced, centered, and in harmony with life. When our gift of thought is operating in this free-flowing way, our experience of life is always rich, full, and deeply satisfying.

In such healthy states of mind, human beings don't experience themselves as "things" or "objects" separate from the rest of life. They don't show up as "egos" or "self-images." In fact, when our divine gift of thought shifts into healthy gear, the experiences of "self-ishness" and "self-consciousness" instantly disappear!

Healthy Children are Great Examples

Healthy children haven't yet learned to significantly interfere with the natural, healthy operation of their divine gift of thought. Thus, they don't go to bed or wake up in the middle of the night wondering, "Who am I?" They don't think much about trying to improve their "self-image." They don't go around searching for their "true identity." Healthy children seldom experience themselves as "self-concepts," "egos," or "fixed personalities."

Please recall your typical experience of life when you were a healthy child. Can you remember how you made up games? As a child, creative ideas for games and adventures just occurred to you, seemingly from out of the blue. Most of the time, you fully savored each moment of life and novel ideas for games just popped into your head. It didn't take any effort, it just happened, naturally.

When I was about seven years old, I can remember creating a spaceship with some friends in the area under the stairs leading to our basement. First, we draped blankets and sheets to cover the sides. At the end, an old tube-type vacuum cleaner became our rocket engine. I was Tom Corbet, space cadet. My friends were my shipmates, Astro and Manning. Together we explored several galaxies and solar systems long before Captain Kirk and the Star Trek crew made the scene. We were totally absorbed in our imaginary adventures and enjoyed most every moment. We hardly ever got bored with our games, and often kept them alive for days on end. We continued playing until we were struck by a fresh thought. Instantly, a new game was created.

When I was about six or so, I remember digging a small, round hole in my backyard, may eight inches in diameter. Then I moved about a hundred yards away and using a baseball bat as a golf club, I hit a softball toward the hole until it finally rolled in. I imagined that I was Arnold Palmer on the pro tour. I made putts worth thousands of dollars as the crowd cheered. I did this for hours on end. I enjoyed every whack of the ball and every walk toward the hole. I wasn't committed to the thought that it was better for the ball to be in the hole than a hundred yards away. Missing a shot was as much fun as making one. I was fully immersed in the process of playing.

As a child, I was typically open-minded and could change the nature of my games in an instant. Since my innate healthy thinking oozed flexibility, having rigid rules for games didn't seem to make much sense. For example, it didn't really matter to me that my golf club was a bat, or that I had no real golf balls, or that the hole was too big, or that there was no putting green on my course. I was just present in the moment, enjoying the rich, healthy experience of living that my divine gift of thought was effortlessly creating.

When our "identity illusions" were small and our healthy functioning big, the games in our lives served as structures or clearings in which to express our natural joy and creativity. The particular game didn't really matter. Each served as a vessel or container to be filled with our natural creativity and self-expression. Our innate, healthy psychological functioning filled up these game containers like a liquid or a gas fills up vessels of different shapes and sizes. When one was filled, we simply invented another and began filling it.

Our futile search for a "true self" began to occur when the dial of our thinking got jarred away from its natural, healthy station or frequency, and the interference or static started getting real loud. I'm suggesting that over time, it's likely that you, like me, inadvertently learned to short-circuit your gift of thought. By so doing, you started losing the rich, clear signal from the natural station or source of your birthright of healthy mental functioning. Wouldn't it be wonderful to get this signal tuned back in once again on a regular basis?

Through understanding the principles of Psychology of Mind, you can learn how to free your innate gift of thought from the noise and static that has kept it from working predominantly in its natural, quiet, effortless way. With a shift in understanding, you can release the higher quality psychological perspectives that were meant to be your normal life experience. I invite you to attend a reunion with your natural human design to live in the typical experience of high quality psychological functioning.

Your Birthright of Effortless Mental Health

Most of you know that you were born with a physical immune system that's designed to protect you from disease and mobilize your body's natural healing forces when you're physically ill. You didn't have to do anything to get this profound physical gift other than be born a human being. This resilient capacity for physical health and natural healing is your human birthright. If you nurture it with good habits like a sensible diet and proper exercise, and avoid bad habits like smoking and excessive stress, it will automatically and effortlessly keep you physically healthy most of the time.

Every now and then, of course, you might catch a cold or get the flu. However, if you rest and take care of yourself, your natural biological immune system will automatically kick in and bring you back to health in no time. Occasionally, you may need some medical attention. Yet, most physicians will tell you that just about everything they do simply helps to empower, bolster, or free up your body's natural immune capacity so that it can bring you back to health.

You were born with this incredibly resilient capacity for healthy physical functioning. Even if you abuse your body for years with bad physical habits, there's still a good chance that you can bounce back to health if you're willing to curtail the destructive habits that have blocked your immune system from doing its natural job.

Please consider the following questions. If we were all created with a natural capacity to experience good physical health most of the time, why would we be designed any differently for psychological functioning or mental health? You were born with a natural biological design to keep you in good physical health. Why then would you be born in a state of psychological imbalance and have to search your whole life for a few precious moments of happiness and inner peace? What an absurd and cruel joke that would be. I don't know about your creator or higher power, but I don't think mine would play such a lousy trick on me!

Yet, when I reflected on how my life used to look, as well as the current lives of so many other people, that was exactly the condition that appeared to exist. Before my understanding breakthroughs, my physical health and mental health were worlds apart. Most of my life, say ninety to ninety-five percent of the time, I was physically well with no major aches, pains, or illnesses.

Except for the few occasions when I had the flu, a cold, or a headache, I hardly ever noticed or thought much about my body or physical health. It was just there, virtually invisible in the background, operating superbly, fully supporting me in all of my physical activities and pursuits.

Psychologically, however, almost the opposite was true. Before my level of understanding shifted, I spent about five, maybe ten percent of my life feeling really good psychologically...about the same amount of time I spent feeling physically ill! In those days, most of my life was spent in various levels of psychological stress or dis-ease. Then, I noticed my mental health, or lack of it, much of the time. Some days were better than others. Most of the time, however, I felt various amounts of tension or stress and did my best to cope with these annoying feelings. Back then, my experience of healthy psychological functioning was much more the exception than the rule.

Clearly, all human beings are born with a built-in natural capacity for good physical health. This resilient capacity is designed to keep us healthy unless it gets overridden or short-circuited by bad physical habits. Why then wouldn't we be born with a similar capacity for healthy psychological functioning? Well, the only sensible answer seems obvious. I propose that you, me, all human beings, are born with a natural design to live in healthy psychological functioning most of the time. Every person is born with a powerful, resilient, natural design to live typically in high quality psychological experiences. Left to its own devices, our innate human design for healthy mental functioning will effortlessly produce high levels of satisfaction and fulfillment, the ability to savor and enjoy the experience of living, and the capacity to engage in life in truly peaceful and contented ways most of the time.

Again, healthy children serve as wonderful examples. They spend most of their time just being themselves, little human beings thinking mostly in a natural way. Thus, they show up immersed in high quality states of mental functioning most of the time. Most mornings, they wake up exhilarated and inspired. They seem to have boundless energy. They tend to learn effortlessly and absorb knowledge intuitively like sponges. Usually, they express themselves fully, show love and affection unconditionally, and dance and sing with little hesitation. In her wonderful book, *Tinkerbell Jerusalem*, Bonnie Kelley Kaback describes her joyous experience as a child at Christmas time.

>"My favorite spot was under the tree, lying with my head between the presents, my legs splayed out from under a pink flannel nightgown, my feet wiggling in little white wool socks. I blurred my eyes, turned the multi-colored lights into stars, and watched their reflections on round, multi-colored balls.

>I stayed there for hours, dreaming of a fantasy land where every day was Christmas, every breeze smelled like pine, and everything was coated in sugar."

The bottom line is this. Please stop trying to build up your ego and self-concept. They're not who you truly are. Please stop living life as if you were a fixed personality...it's not the real you! Please stop searching out there for your "true self." Now you know the truth. **Who you truly are is a human being with the divine gift of thought designed to operate automatically in a healthy way with absolutely no effort from you. How good can you stand it!**

Chapter 4

Measuring the Quality of Your Mental Health

H ere are a few more questions for you to ponder. If who you really are is a human being with the divine gift of thought designed to operate automatically in a health-producing way most of the time...then how well are you functioning these days? To what extent is your remarkable gift of thought operating in the natural, quiet way it was designed to operate? How much time are you typically spending in the neighborhood of high quality psychological functioning? In other words, how often are you being your true self?

"List A" - The Neighborhood of Genuine Mental Health

Let's examine once again that list of high quality psychological experiences that we visited in Chapter Three. This time I've called it, "List A." The items on List A represent the healthy psychological experiences that all human beings have when their divine gift of thought is operating according to its natural design principles. I could compose a similar list of high quality physical experiences that all people have when their biological systems are functioning in their innate, healthy way. For example, when people's physical systems are working efficiently, they have a body temperature of around 98.6 degrees, a blood pressure in the vicinity of 120/80, lots of energy, and minimal aches and pains. The items on List A describe how human beings typically experience life when they're thinking in the high quality, natural way that they were designed to think most of the time.

When our gift of thought is operating in sync with its natural design principles, we automatically find ourselves in the high quality psychological experiences represented by List A. List A is the psychological community that every human being instantly accesses when their gift of thought is operating in its intended way. A person's age, gender, ethnicity, religion, skin color, profession, political affiliation, sexual orientation, or income level has absolutely nothing to do with the quality of their psychological functioning or mental health. List A represents the high quality psychological experiences that all human beings have to some degree when their divine gift of thought is operating in its natural, effortless way.

It's helpful to measure how efficiently your gift of thought typically functions. It's useful to recognize the "normal" quality level of your thinking...to gauge how frequently your gift of thought is operating in the quiet, invisible way it was designed to operate. Why? Because by so doing, you can see how much time you typically spend being your true self.

Here's how to do it. Please review the items on List A and put a check mark in the column that best describes the amount of time you typically spend experiencing each one. Please don't check the time you spend searching for each item, thinking about each item, reading about each item, or pretending about each item. Simply check the frequency category that approximates the time you actually spend experiencing each one. Finally, give yourself an overall rating for the time you spend being your true self...a human being thinking in an effortless, high quality way. Please don't worry about your results. It's just a game designed to help you move toward some breakthroughs in understanding.

"List A"
Healthy Psychological Functioning

	Most of the time	A lot of the time	Some of the time	Seldom	Hardly ever
A calm, peaceful mind					
Free-flowing, effortless thinking					
Stress-free productivity					
Ability to focus and concentrate without effort					
Experiencing life as an interesting adventure					
Motivated by curiosity and inspiration					
More fully present in each moment					
Feeling content, satisfied, and fulfilled					
Heightened sense of humor					
Relaxed, at ease, easy to be with					
High capacity for insight and creativity					
Focus is on the beauty in life					
Happy with the way things are					
Common sense, appropriate behavior					
Kindness, joy, generosity					

	Most of the time	A lot of the time	Some of the time	Seldom	Hardly ever
Focus on enjoyment, light-hearted					
Empathy, compassion understanding					
Cooperation, flexibility, open-minded					
Optimistic, positive attitude					
Learning from mistakes and moving on					
Love, gratitude, and intimacy					
In love with life					

**Time Spent Being
Your True Self**

Let's examine your responses. How often did you check the "most of the time" and "a lot of the time" categories? If most of your ratings fell in these columns, it would appear that your divine gift of thought is typically operating in the natural, healthy way it was designed to operate. Much of the time you're already thinking in the quiet, effortless way that naturally produces high quality psychological perspectives. Congratulations! You're being your true self much of the time these days.

I request, however, that you stay with us on our journey. Why? Because I'm confident that you can move to an even higher level of understanding about your psychological functioning. Through deepening your present level of understanding, you'll likely find that you've just touched the surface of what's possible in the realm of your incredible human potential. By continuing to listen with a quiet mind, it's quite possible that you will unleash much more of your natural human intelligence and boundless human spirit!

If most of your ratings fell in the "some of the time," "seldom," or "hardly ever" categories, it would appear that much of the time, your divine gift of thought isn't operating in its natural, quiet, high quality way. Thus, you're not typically having the full, rich experience of life that your thinking ability was designed to produce for you most of the time. Please don't be discouraged...it's not your fault. With a shift in understanding, you'll see how you innocently learned to misuse your thinking and short-circuit the natural operation of your divine gift of thought. With a breakthrough in understanding, you'll instantly recognize how to access the source of residing in List A as a way of life.

"List B" -The Mental Flu Symptoms Scale

Now, let's examine a second group of items. I've called this one, "List B." The items on List B represent the many and varied symptoms of the "mental flu." List B items represent varying degrees of mental fever and dis-ease that occur for people when their gift of thought isn't operating in sync with its natural design principles. These items illustrate the lower quality psychological experiences that occur for people when they start misusing their thinking. By completing this scale, you can begin to recognize the amount of time that you spend innocently overriding or short-circuiting the healthy operation of your gift of thought.

As you did for List A, please estimate the time you typically spend <u>experiencing</u> each item on List B. Then give yourself an overall rating for the amount of time you're spending not being your true self.

"List B"
Mental Flu Symptoms Scale

	Most of the time	A lot of the time	Some of the time	Seldom	Hardly ever
Busy mind: computer-like analytical thinking					
Need to prove yourself - "ego" and "self-image" tend to dominate					
Pride and excitement about winning, being right, and looking good					
Feeling secure when needs, wants, and desires are met					
Preoccupied with the past or future					
Mind tends to worry, or find fault					
Motivated by achievement and competition					
Impatience, frustration, hurriedness					
Focus on how life could be better					
Boredom, restlessness, dissatisfaction					
Defensiveness, conflict, misunderstandings					
Dwelling on mistakes and repeating them					
Effort, drudgery, strain					
Conflict and incompatibility					
Blame, judgment, self-righteousness					

	Most of the time	A lot of the time	Some of the time	Seldom	Hardly ever
Stress, burnout, anxiety, inefficiency					
Negative attitude - closed and prejudiced					
Emotional instability					
Sadness, sorrow, depression					
Anger, grudges, hostility					
Revenge, paranoia, violence					
Hate, prejudice					

**Time Spent Not
Being Your True Self**

Let's take a moment to highlight some specific items on List B. It's interesting to notice that many people in this culture have learned to think that certain List B items, like being motivated by achievement and competition, having a strong "ego" and "self-image," living with a busy, computer-like mind, and experiencing stress and boredom, represent normal, even healthy levels of psychological functioning. Also, many people have been taught that it's a healthy sign to feel emotions like pride and excitement connected to winning, being right, and looking good. Many others have come to believe that it's normal to have their experience of well-being and security attached to the satisfaction of their needs, wants, and desires. A lot people think that it's natural to live with a certain amount of stress, turmoil, conflict, and discontent in their lives.

Also, many people seem to respect and even seek out certain List B feelings like sadness, sorrow, and depression. These people think that such negative feelings somehow build character, gratitude or strength. For example, how often have you heard someone say,

"How can you appreciate the good feelings in life if you don't have the bad ones to compare them to?"

It's helpful to recognize that many of the psychological experiences that people in this culture have learned to see as "normal" or helpful are actually symptoms of psychological malfunctioning or the mental flu! Please look over each List B item one more time. Read them slowly, one by one. Consider the fact that each of the mental experiences on List B is the psychological counterpart of a physical disease symptom! All of the items on List B represent symptoms of lower quality psychological functioning or varying degrees of psychological hacking, wheezing, retching, and ralfing!

With this fact in mind, please reflect on our typical television soap operas and talk shows. Do they tend to showcase List A items, or items from List B? How about the news media... List A or List B? The political arena... List A or List B? The movies... List A or List B? Your psychotherapist... List A or List B? Your company or work place... List A or List B?   Your family...List A or List B? Yourself... List A or List B? If you answered "List B" to several or most of these questions, it's likely that you're beginning to see that we live in a culture that has misguidedly become preoccupied and fascinated with the symptoms of the mental flu. Our culture has innocently come to view many of these symptoms as signs of "normal," even healthy psychological functioning.

Please remember, the purpose of completing List A and List B was to nudge your awareness...to help you see the extent to which you've innocently learned to misuse your thinking in a way that overrides or short-circuits the natural, efficient, effortless operation of your gift of thought. Remember, when your thinking is working in the quiet, natural way it was designed to work, it instantly, effortlessly, and automatically moves you somewhere in the neighborhood of List A.

Perhaps you're wondering at this point, "If I was born with a divine gift of thought, and the natural capacity for it to function in a healthy way...what happened? How did I begin drifting away from the typical experience of a List A life? What's behind this insidious process? What caused this unfortunate transformation? How did my natural, healthy thinking capacity become overridden or short-circuited so often? How can I free it up to work more consistently in its natural, high quality way? Where do I begin?"

Congratulations...these are great questions! Your willingness to ask them or even consider them means that you're already on your way to higher levels of understanding. Please remember, a shift in understanding is all that it takes. With a breakthrough in understanding, your divine gift of thought will automatically start working more frequently in its natural health-producing way. How good can you stand it!

Chapter 5

Understanding Your Psychological Functioning

E very semester, I ask the students in my university classes the same question. To this day, I haven't found one that was certain of the answer. In fact, most don't seem to have a clue. The question I ask them is this, "How many of you clearly understand the true cause or source of every one of your feelings, perceptions, and behaviors?" If pressed for an answer, some students will mention the past, child-rearing, temperament, personality traits, or heredity. Few, however, can get very specific.

What's even more astounding is that even most of our best trained "mind mechanics" don't accurately understand how human beings work psychologically. At last count, over two hundred different perspectives on human psychological functioning had been proposed by the mental health community! Each of these models offers a different set of causes for psychological dysfunction, and suggests a different approach to prevention and treatment. Can you imagine your chances of getting your sick car running smoothly again if there were over two hundred different views on how to repair the exact same engine? At best, most of today's "mind mechanics" can help you cope better with life in your broken down state. At worst, they can add a few more degrees to your mental fever!

Why is it so important that people accurately understand how they work psychologically? Well, for one thing, if you don't understand your own mental functioning, you're likely to spend considerable time being confused, perplexed, even frightened and deluded by it. For example, you're not going to understand your moods, your inconsistencies, your crazy thoughts, the range of your emotions and feelings, your needs, wants, urges, or your self-defeating habits and behaviors. More importantly, you're not going to understand what true psychological health really is, where it comes from, and how to release more of it on a regular basis.

The "More, Better, Different" Game

When people don't understand their mental functioning, they're likely to live much of their lives gripped by the illusion that the quality of life is determined by outside sources. Likewise, they will tend to experience their feelings, perceptions, and behavior being caused by outside circumstances. When people don't clearly know how they work psychologically, it's much more likely that they'll perceive other people and outside events as the cause or source of the quality of their moment to moment experience of life.

What happens next? Well, when people experience the quality of their life being determined by externals, they spend much of their time tinkering with themselves and things out there. They get caught up in the vicious circle of what's been called the "more, better, different" game. Here's how it works. People misguidedly think that they'll be happier if they can get more of certain things in their lives (e.g., money), or if they can get better in certain areas of their lives (e.g., parenting), or if they can do certain things in their lives differently (e.g., change jobs).

Unfortunately, this often compulsive process can never lead to   true,   sustained   happiness.   Ego   highs...maybe,   identity illusions...always, genuine fulfillment...never!   Most people don't realize this, however.   Why?   Because most people don't clearly understand how they work psychologically.   Therefore, when their first round of tinkering doesn't work that well, they try again.   In the next round, they might do more of the things they're already doing better, or they might try to get better at the things they're already doing differently, or perhaps they'll try to get more of the things they want in a slightly different way...and so on, and so on, and so on, and so on!

When people don't realize how they work psychologically, they tend to keep going down empty tunnel after empty tunnel. Why are these tunnels so often empty?   Because you can't live consistently in the neighborhood of List A by doing "more, better, or different" of anything external.   Happiness doesn't come from out there.   Its natural source is within each of us.   It automatically shows up when our divine gift of thought is working in its inherent, healthy way.   Because their level of understanding is low, however, most people never find the sustained happiness, well-being, and peace of mind they're after.   Thus, too many people misguidedly spend most of their lives tinkering with the stuff in their List B empty tunnels!

Can you blame people for this misguided behavior?   Of course not.   Why?   Because when people don't clearly understand how they work psychologically, it really appears to them that true happiness can be found by manipulating externals.   Really!   Even when people get an inkling that they might be misinformed about the true source of genuine happiness, it's hard for most to follow that "calling."   Why?   Well, for one thing, most people have stopped trusting the signals from their natural wisdom and common sense when they happen to occur.   Not understanding and trusting this natural intelligence, combined with seeing so many others still fully engaged in the "more, better, different" game, most people think, "What if my inkling is wrong and my friends get there before I do?"   With limited understanding of human psychological functioning, most people aren't moved by the occasional insights that reveal the futility of their effortful tinkering!

It's helpful to stop tinkering and allow your present level of understanding to shift upward. Please remember, unleashing more of your birthright of healthy mental functioning doesn't require effort, struggle, or tinkering of any kind. You don't have to change anything external, like your job, your spouse, other people, or any of the circumstances in your life. You don't have to do more, better, or different of anything out there.

Also, you can't release your natural happiness by deliberately tinkering with the thoughts stored in your memory. Deliberately playing with the thoughts you've picked up along the way can't lead you back to your birthright of healthy mental functioning. Many of these memories are very useful, but they're not designed to unleash your natural happiness and peace of mind.

Thought Recognition

Just what will take you back to a predominantly List A life? The key to spending more time in List A is what Psychology of Mind calls "thought recognition." Simply put, thought recognition is recognizing the role that thought plays in producing your moment to moment experience of life. Thought recognition requires a shift in understanding from which you can see how your every life experience is created through the miracle of thought.

When you discover how thought works to create your on-going personal experience of life, you'll be empowered to access at will, the natural thinking ability that will automatically move you into the neighborhood of List A. With thought recognition, you'll allow your divine gift of thought to effortlessly release more of your innate human intelligence, wisdom, creativity, and genuine happiness. Please get ready for the hands-on owner's manual for understanding the healthy operation and maintenance of your gift of thought...the one they didn't give you or your parents when you came down the chute!

A Quick Reminder Before We Proceed

Before we move on, however, I'd like to remind you once again to listen to what's coming in the most effective way. How you listen is so critical to having a breakthrough in understanding...I'd like your permission to review. First, please try to avoid deliberately looking for the answers to happiness. Now that you've heard that the next stop on our journey is understanding exactly how human beings work psychologically, you may find yourself deliberately trying to find some more happiness answers, tools, or techniques to put in your memory. In other words, you may get the urge to start analyzing, and using the following psychological principles like a formula or set of rules for getting to happiness.

Please be very cautious here. Deliberately listening to what's coming through your intellect or analytical thinking will only get you the booby prize! Why? Because at best, if you listen to what's coming by deliberately processing it through the information in your memory, you'll just come up with a "more, better, or different" version of what you already know. At worst, you'll start judging and evaluating what's coming and making yourself right. Well, guess what? You'll get to be right and you'll miss the jackpot. The sheer noise of your effortful, analytical thinking will prevent you from hearing a breakthrough.

What's the best way to listen here? Again, please keep listening in what Psychology of Mind calls a "reflective listening mode." Very simply, this means listening with a calm, non-analytical, judgment-free mind. Keep listening for <u>not</u> knowing. Take on the mind set that it's not important to deliberately process or analyze what's coming. Simply quiet your mind. Trust it to listen for you without any effort or struggle on your part, whatsoever.

Please don't hold onto or "squeeze " any thoughts that happen to cross your mind. Pretend that your mind is coated with Teflon and that your thoughts can do nothing but slide through one after the other. You can't have a breakthrough while you're entertaining or processing layer upon layer of thoughts that you've learned along the way. If you're willing to listen with a calm, clear mind, these "insight blockers" will just float by and you'll be much more likely to have a sudden shift in understanding. Remember, breakthroughs require a peaceful, passive mind...not a busy, active one. The bottom line...there's nothing to do but clear your mind and make room for some "ah hah's" to occur! How good can you stand it!

Chapter 6

The Principles of Psychology
of Mind

To help you experience the principles of Psychology of Mind, I'd like to ask you to use your imagination. Here's my request. For a few moments, please pretend that you're a giant movie projector. That's right...for the purpose of catching on to the principles of POM, please imagine that you're an animated, theater-size movie projector...the star of a brand new Walt Disney cartoon.

Take a few moments to get into character. Ready...here we go. First, please visualize your main parts...a powerful, stream-lined motor, a state of the art projection light, and two huge film reels. Now imagine yourself, the movie projector, plugging your cord into a power outlet. Very good. Okay, please move your ignition switch to the "on" position. Wow! Your brilliant projection light is beaming out into space.

Now, Mr. or Ms. Projector, I'd like to ask you to reflect on some important aspects of your movie projector functioning.

First...as a movie projector, what would your experience of life be like if only your projection light was operational? If your powerful beam of projected light was the only source of your experience of life, how do you think life would appear to you?

Please think about it for a minute. Wouldn't it seem reasonable to assume that in this state of movie projector functioning, your experience of life would be something like being engulfed in a vast, endless, formless sea of light? In every direction you looked, there would only be light. In this state of movie projector functioning, you wouldn't see any distinctions or boundaries...no figures, no forms, no shapes...only light. You wouldn't even know that it was "light" surrounding you. Yet, this experience would be everything there was for you in life. With your power source activated and only your brilliant projection light beaming outward, your experience of life would be boundless and formless. Put another way, your life experience in this state of projector functioning would be "everything" and "nothing" (no things or form) at exactly the same time.

Next...what would have to be added to your projector functioning to enable you to experience some objects, things, figures, forms...some distinctions or boundaries in your experience of life? That's right...you'd have to add film. With some film turning on your reels and your projection light beaming, you would then project outward onto your life screen the images, pictures, color, and sound present on each frame of film. Instantly, with film added, your experience of life would have some form, definition, or meaning.

Please try this question. As a movie projector, do you think that you would clearly understand your projector functioning or exactly how you worked? For example, would you know the exact source or cause of the forms, pictures, and images on your screen? Well, if you happened to be a movie projector with a low level of understanding, it might appear to you that the source or cause of the pictures that you were experiencing was somewhere out there on the screen. On the other hand, if you were a naturally wise machine, or had read, *Falling In Love With Life for Movie Projectors*, you would likely understand that the pictures and images on your screen were always being activated from within you. You would know that every picture that came to life on your screen was the result of projecting your light through the images on each frame of your film. While it might appear to a movie projector with a lower level of "film recognition" that the source of her pictures was somewhere out there on the screen, you would clearly understand that your moment to moment experience of life was always being generated within you, from the inside-out!

Here are a few final questions for you, the awakened movie projector. Assume that your projection light had burned out, yet some film was still turning on your reels. What, then, would be your experience of life? Very good. Without a functioning projection light, your experience of life would be nothing...you wouldn't have any. Rotating film, without a light to bring it to life, won't produce any pictures or images on a screen. As a movie projector, your energized motor empowers your projection light to bring the images on your film to life, thus creating your moment to moment life experience from the inside-out.

At any given moment, would the forms, images, or pictures on your screen be the "absolute" reality? In other words, would any momentary pictures that you were projecting onto your screen be the absolute truth? Of course not. Each projected frame of film would produce just one momentary image, one "reality illusion" of many possible ones, depending on the images, color, and sound on that particular frame of film. With different film turning on your reels, you'd project out a much different reality. No particular frame of film filled with light and projected outward would ever produce an absolute reality. Each projected film frame simply creates only one momentary illusion of reality.

As a movie projector, if you were crystal clear about how you functioned, would this understanding help you to have a happier, more peaceful life experience? It's likely that it would. Why? Well, for one thing, you would clearly recognize that in each moment, your experience of life was always being created by you from the inside-out. Thus, you would rarely, if ever, be at the effect of or become gripped by the temporary reality illusions that happened to appear on your screen. You wouldn't take any of them too seriously or become frightened by them. You'd be less apt to identify with or dwell on any of them. Why? Because you would understand that they were all just fleeting reality illusions that automatically change as your next frame of film runs through.

Furthermore, it would be perfectly clear to you why your projector buddies often saw life much differently than you. This fact wouldn't confuse or upset you. You wouldn't fight or struggle with them to prove that the way you saw things was the right way. Why? Because you would know that they were simply projecting different frames of film. You would realize that what movie projectors call reality is always their next film frame.

Every now and then, however, you might temporarily become out of focus. I hear this is quite common, even for movie projectors with high levels of "film recognition." During those times, the quality of the pictures on your screen would be poorer...the images fuzzy and blurred, and the sound perhaps monotone and tinny. With high "film recognition," however, you wouldn't become unsettled or disturbed by these lower quality projections. You wouldn't panic and start struggling to fix them. You wouldn't be tempted to cope by racing to the theater concession stand and pigging out on popcorn and candy. No, understanding your projector functioning, you'd realize that it was just a mood...just some momentary lower quality projections. Thus, you'd likely relax and allow your automatic focusing mechanism to quietly kick in and do its job. Soon, your projections would be crisp and clear once again.

Human Beings Work a Lot Like Movie Projectors

Thanks for playing along. Hopefully, this imagination exercise will help you better understand your human psychological functioning. Why? Because according to Psychology of Mind, in some significant ways, human beings work in a manner quite similar to movie projectors. According to POM, for human beings, our **Mind** is comparable to a movie projector's motor and power source.   Our faculty of **Consciousness** is analogous to a movie projector's light beam.   The film?   For human beings, the film, of course, is **Thought**.

Mind, **Consciousness**, and **Thought** are the three major principles of Psychology of Mind.   According to POM, these three psychological elements or mental building blocks work together to produce every human psychological experience.   Within these principles are the answers to mankind's deepest questions about the mystery of human life.   Let's examine each one very closely.

Psychological Building Block # 1: Mind

According to POM, "Mind" (like the energized projector motor) is the power source behind our ability to think.   Our mind enables us to produce mental images, pictures, and other representations of the world in our head.   Also, our mind is the source of our faculty of "Consciousness."   Consciousness (like the movie projector's light beam) is the capacity of human beings to create experience from thought.   Consciousness brings our thoughts to life and makes them appear real to us.   Similar to a movie projector, POM proposes that our mind mixes our thoughts (psychological film) with our faculty of consciousness (psychological projection light) to produce our unique, on-going, moment to moment experience of life.

What are the products or results of this continuous mixing of thoughts with consciousness by the mind?   In other words, what kind of items do human beings experience on their psychological screen?   What are the products of our projected thoughts in action? These experiences include all of our feelings and emotions from outrage to gratitude, each of our perceptions or how everything looks to us, from delusional to pristine, and all of our reactions and behaviors including everything we say and do, from wise to destructive.   According to Psychology of Mind, the source of every human psychological experience is thought brought to life by the faculty of consciousness.

Psychological Building Block # 2: Consciousness

Consciousness is similar to the projection light of a movie projector. It is the capacity of human beings to create experience from thought. It is the agency that brings our thoughts to life and makes them appear real to us. If we didn't have the faculty of consciousness, we wouldn't experience anything at all. Like film running through a movie projector with a burned out projection light, there would be nothing on our psychological screen without the faculty of consciousness.

Consciousness alone, however, isn't enough. Thought has to be mixed with consciousness to create the on-going illusion of reality. If the film clip with the images on it is thought, then the light that makes the film clip visible is consciousness. Each person's reality is constantly being formed in this way. Thus, each person "knows" a life that is uniquely generated moment to moment through thought plus consciousness.

Consciousness makes our thoughts appear real to us through our five senses; sight, hearing, touch, smell, and taste. What we "know" becomes experienced as real in each moment via these senses. To experience this process in action, please try one more brief imagination process.   First, hold out one of your hands. Thank you. Now imagine that I'm placing a large, ripe, bright, yellow lemon in that hand. Please feel the shape of the lemon. Notice the smooth, waxy feel of the skin. Now bring the lemon up to your nose the smell the rind. Notice the faint lemony smell? Now please hold out your other hand. Careful...I'm handing you a very sharp butcher knife. Please don't cut yourself! Okay, now place the juicy lemon on a flat surface and very quickly slice it in half. Look out...some of the tart lemon juice just missed your eye. Now bring the exposed pulp of the fat, juicy lemon to your nose and take a nice big whiff. Quickly, take a big bite of tart, glittering pulp from the plump, dripping lemon and savor the tangy, sour taste.

What you just experienced was your own thoughts in action. You just experienced the result of your consciousness bringing your thoughts to life through your senses. There was no actual lemon in this experiment, only "lemon thought."   Your faculty of consciousness brought your memories of the smell, feel, and taste of an imaginary lemon to life for you. It was your faculty of consciousness that activated these thoughts through your senses of touch, taste, and smell.

By the way, if this example didn't work that well for you...please imagine the screech of some dry chalk on a blackboard or that you're sliding down a long banister that suddenly turns into a razor blade! Sorry...I just want you to experience the idea.

There are many other poignant illustrations of the principle of consciousness.   For example, people suffering from post-traumatic stress disorder like war veterans or violent crime victims often experience flashbacks in which the "traumatic" event they once endured appears to be happening all over again.   When the memories of such events get reactivated, the original feelings, visions, and bodily movements can be re-experienced.

People with psychosomatic disorders can experience extreme pain or even paralysis in a limb for which there is absolutely no valid physical or anatomical explanation. For these people, their thoughts carry the message of pain to their senses when pain isn't actually being caused physically. On the other hand, most everyone knows that "real" pain can be reduced or even eliminated if our minds are distracted from it. That's how hypnosis works to create a "psychological anesthetic" for dental procedures or how Lamaze training works for childbirth. To the degree that people don't think about pain, their consciousness doesn't project thoughts of pain to their senses.

In the equation of human psychological functioning, mind and consciousness are both constants. This means that whatever thoughts happen to be moving through our mind will automatically be brought to life by our consciousness and become our psychological reality in that moment. Likewise, our consciousness will make any thoughts appear real to us when they are subjected to the illumination that consciousness provides.

As long as we're alive, our mind and our consciousness will keep doing their respective jobs, and there's absolutely nothing we can do about it.   There is, however, one element of our psychological functioning about which we do have a say. This is the element of thought. From the standpoint of spending more time in the neighborhood of List A, understanding the principle of Thought is a major key. How good can you stand it!

■

Chapter 7

Thought: The Key Building Block

I t's very helpful to realize that as a human being, you're constantly thinking. Every minute of every hour, every hour of every day of your entire life, your thoughts are always in motion. Each instant, your mind is producing a waterfall of thoughts. Even while you're sleeping, you're always thinking. Dreams are simply more reels of thought being brought to life by your consciousness and projected onto your sleeping screen.

Sometimes, our thinking shows up like a chattering little voice in our head that's actively commenting, remembering, analyzing, judging, criticizing, justifying, and theorizing. In fact, many people have gotten so used to thinking primarily in this noisy, effortful, more deliberate way, they hardly notice it anymore. How about you? Please take a few moments to check in on your thinking. Take about thirty seconds and listen to your thinking very carefully. Notice if it's quiet and peaceful in there, or whether you can hear a little thought voice chattering away.

(Please listen to your thinking for thirty seconds)

Well, what was it like in there? Was it peaceful and still, or did you hear some noisy, chattering thinking going on? If you're confused or not sure, please let me coach your awareness. Perhaps it was the little voice in your head that said something like, "What voice? I don't hear any chattering little thought voice. What's he talking about? This is crazy!"

At times, this more deliberate, chattering, processing type of thinking will quiet down or even disappear. During those times, the quality of our thinking changes markedly. It becomes virtually effortless, flows quietly, and operates invisibly in the background.

Whichever way your thoughts tend to be formed, they are always in motion as long as you're alive. Experiencing a breakthrough in understanding about the principle of thought, and the ways in which your thoughts can be produced, is the key to residing in the neighborhood of List A as a way of life.

What We Call "Reality," is Always Our Thoughts in Action

Most people have a low level of thought recognition. Thus, it typically appears to most people that what they're experiencing on their psychological screen is happening to them from the outside-in. The truth, however, is just the opposite. Everything that appears to be happening "out there" on the screen is actually being created within us, from the inside-out. Every psychological event that we have, every "reality illusion" that we experience, is always the product of our thoughts brought to life by our faculty of consciousness. In each and every moment, we always experience a unique version of reality created by our own activated thoughts. What we call "reality," is always our thoughts in action!

Please consider the following illustration. Take a moment and look around the room you're in right now. You can probably see some windows, walls, a door, some lights, furniture, a floor, and a ceiling. It's helpful to understand that everything you see in your room is actually an illusion created by your own consciousness-activated thoughts. Each window, door, wall, light, floor, and ceiling in your room looks the way it does to you solely because of your thoughts in action. You see each of the objects in your room the way you do because you've learned the particular thoughts that, when brought to life through your senses, allow you to see them that way. If you didn't have those thoughts stored in your memory, you couldn't see any of these objects the way that you do.

When you were an infant, for example, your crib could have been in this exact same room and you wouldn't have seen any windows, doors, lights, etc. Why? Because you hadn't yet stored the thoughts in your memory necessary to create these particular reality illusions. It was only after you added such thoughts to your memory that your faculty of consciousness could arrange the "physicalness" of your room in a way that had windows, doors, walls, lights, floor, and a ceiling appear.

Interestingly, once we start habitually processing the particular memories that create our unique view of things, it's often difficult to see our personal reality illusions in any other way. For example, once you've gotten used to activating the thoughts that create the reality illusions of doors, windows, lights, etc., it's likely that you innocently began to think that they really were those things!

Please look at it this way. Imagine that you could ask a fish in an aquarium some questions about the water in his tank. If the fish could talk, it's likely that he'd say, "What water? I don't see any water!" The fish, you see, has gotten so used to living in water that he doesn't even realize it's there. The same thing is true for most of us humans. Most of us have gotten so used to living in the sea of experiences created by our own thoughts in action that we don't realize that it's our thoughts creating them. Thus, most people don't understand that objects like chairs, windows, lights, floors, and ceilings exist for them the way they do solely because of their personal, activated thoughts.

At first, this very useful distinction can be a little tricky to get. In the beginning, most people find it difficult to comprehend that <u>every</u> experience they have in life is <u>always</u> created from the inside-out by their own thoughts. It's empowering to understand that <u>everything</u> in your life, including the chairs, windows, doors, walls, floor, and ceiling in your room, is a product of your thoughts in action. It's very helpful to understand that someone else with different memories would experience the "physicalness" of your room in an entirely different way.

If you will, please consider the following demonstration. Imagine that we found an African Bushman, blindfolded him, and transported him from his bush country home all the way to the middle of your favorite room. Upon removing his blindfold, I assert that the Bushman would not see your door, or your windows, or your floor, or your ceiling, or most of the other "obvious to you" items in your room. In fact, if you didn't watch him closely, the Bushman might walk smack into your window and break his nose. Why? Because the Bushman has no stored thoughts for glass or window. Without these memories, it's impossible for the Bushman to see and respond to your "window" and the rest of the physical objects in your room in the same way that you do.

Furthermore, the Bushman wouldn't know how to get out of your room. Why? Because he has no thoughts for a door. Thus, he wouldn't see any door, or know its purpose in your culture. Also, he wouldn't see a floor, a ceiling, walls, or lights, at least not at all like you do. If you could ask him what he saw, he would look through the particular thoughts that he's picked up along the way. His answers would probably sound strange to you. Why? Because the Bushman has some very different thoughts than you stored in the files of his memory.

Did you happen to see the movie, "The Gods Must Be Crazy?" In this critically acclaimed film, a pilot flying a small two-seater over the Australian bush country drops an empty Coca-Cola bottle from his cockpit window. A Bushman hunting on the ground below sees the glittering object fall from the sky and land near his path. Having no thoughts to see a Coke bottle, he is startled and confused by this "strange" thing. Cautiously, he picks it up and puts it in his pack. Hastening back to his village, he proudly displays his find.

For the next several weeks, the tribe members speculate about the origin and purpose of the peculiar object. They finally conclude that it was sent to them by the gods. They invent several purposes for the bottle, using it as a tool for grinding, weaving, and building. Soon, however, jealousies begin to erupt over who will get to use the "sacred" object and for what purpose. The conflict continues to escalate until the tribal chieftain finally decides that the strange object must have really been sent by the evil spirits. The chief then orders the Bushman to take the "Devil's tool" to the end of the earth, and drop it over the side.

This unique film supplies several pointed examples of the phenomenon of experiencing life from the inside-out. It nicely illustrates that nothing, physical or otherwise, has an "absolute" meaning that exists independently of our thoughts. Rather, the particular thoughts brought to life by our consciousness determine our unique experience of each object and circumstance. Every experience we have as a human being is a "thought event."

In New York City, about 15 years ago, 150 representatives to the United Nations from about 50 different countries had just finished the main course at an awards banquet. Unbeknownst to them, some researchers were conducting an experiment to determine how people's thoughts influence their eating behavior. The experiment focused on how each person at the banquet would eat their dessert, a typical, triangular wedge of apple pie. Waiters had been instructed to serve the pie slices in a specific, pre-determined direction in front of each diner. Randomly, the pie wedges were placed in front of each person so that the point of the wedge faced either north, east, or west. The researchers then observed how each guest ate his or her slice of pie.

Here's what happened. Of the 150 guests present, approximately 50 were native Americans. Before taking the first bite of pie, each American guest turned the pie plate so that the point of the wedge was facing toward them. Then, they ate the pie starting from the point and proceeding backward. Virtually all of the remaining 100 non-American guests cut into their pie wedge from whatever direction it happened to be facing. Only the

Americans turned their plates so that the point of the pie wedge was facing them before starting to eat!

Eating a wedge of pie from the tip backwards is not the absolute pie eating reality. It's not the way some deity or higher power proclaimed that humans should eat pie. It's simply the particular "pie-eating thoughts" that most human beings in the American culture have stored in their memory. Thus, when these thoughts are activated, it appears to many Americans that this is the "right" or "true" way to eat a wedge of pie.

I'm told that the Eskimo language contains over fifty words for snow. This shouldn't be too surprising, since snow is so important in the day-to-day life of Eskimos. Their diverse language or multiple thoughts for snow allows Eskimos to see distinctions in snow that you and I could never see. For example, Eskimos can easily distinguish snow that's good for building, good for traveling, good for eating, and good for storage of food. You and I would look and likely see only snow, snow, and more snow!

Likewise, I've heard that an Ethiopian cattle herdsman can scan his entire herd from a great distance and easily discern which cows are ill, which are pregnant, and which are in heat. You and I would look and see cows, cows, and more cows!

Each person continually experiences his own thoughts in action. In each moment, we can see only the particular reality illusion that's being created by our activated thoughts at that moment. As our thoughts change, so does the illusion of reality that we experience. Since no two people have exactly the same thoughts, and no one person has the same thoughts all the time, each of us lives in a unique thought-created reality illusion that's continually changing. What we call reality is always our next thought!

The following illustration may help underscore this helpful distinction. Below are two trapezoids. Within each trapezoid is a well-known, common phrase. Please take a moment and read each of the two phrases.

```
 _____        _____
 \    PARIS      \       /  A BIRD        \
  \   IN THE      \     /   IN THE         \
   \  THE SPRING   \   /    THE HAND        \
    \     XX        \ /        XX            \
     ----------------  ----------------------
```

Very good. Now, please read each phrase once again. Good! Now, read each phrase one more time, starting with the second one first. If you haven't caught on yet, please read each phrase once more. No, it's not the double X's at the bottom of each phrase. Sorry! Read each phrase once again, this time very slowly. Did you get it? If not, please read each one again, this time very, very slowly. If you haven't caught on by now, I request that you read them once more this way. Please put your finger on each word in each phrase, and read them aloud this time. Make sure you point to each word as you say each phrase. Now you've got it! There's a second "the" in both phrases. It's "Paris in the the spring," and "A bird in the the hand."

This is a great example of seeing our thoughts in action. What people see in each trapezoid is their own thoughts. Since most of us have the thought stored in our memory that there should only be one "the" in these common phrases, most of us see only one "the!"

Not seeing a second "the" in some simple phrases is certainly not the end of the world. However, not knowing that we're always seeing our own thoughts in action can needlessly complicate our lives. For example, many of the thoughts we've collected along the way are very selective and biased. To the degree that we start actively processing these less useful thoughts and don't realize what we're doing, we're more likely to become gripped by, or at the effect of, the reality illusions they can produce.

Take Meg, for example, a former client of mine who came to therapy with her boyfriend Sam. Her "issue" was that she couldn't trust men. Meg described several previous relationships, stating that in each one her male partner always did something to violate her trust. Sam, she said, was starting to become just like all the others.

I asked Meg if she could remember the last time she felt trusting feelings toward Sam. She thought for a moment and said, "Well, about two weekends ago we took a short trip and spent the night at this romantic bed and breakfast. Actually, we had a wonderful time. I can even remember thinking that night what a great guy Sam is, and how lucky I am to have him in my life. I really trusted him that night!"

Before I could comment, Meg quickly added that such good times were becoming much less frequent. Sam, she exclaimed, was starting to say and do things that made her very suspicious.

Sam, on the other hand, was at his wit's end. He said he loved Meg very much, but that just about everything he said or did lately was seen by her as either a put-down, or him siding against her. He felt like he was between a rock and a hard place. Even his compliments were regularly misinterpreted as criticisms.

After observing Meg and Sam communicating for just one session, I was crystal clear that Meg had learned to misuse her thinking in a way that often distorted her perspective and interfered with her natural common sense. Meg's lower quality thinking habit, when activated, had her misinterpret and over-react to many of Sam's innocuous statements, gestures, and behaviors. When Meg started thinking in this lower quality way, her thought, "You can't trust men," became her reality. This biased thought in action created a slew of "second the's" about Sam that weren't really there. Unless she began to understand the principle of thought and learned to distinguish her lower quality thinking habit, it was likely that Meg's biased thoughts in action would never let her meet a man that she could trust for very long,

Emotions are Always Our Thoughts in Action

Not only do we always perceive our thoughts in action from moment to moment, we always feel our thoughts in action as well.

Because most people don't clearly understand how they work psychologically, they tend to experience other people and outside circumstances as the source or cause of their feelings. They typically think that negative and positive events determine their emotional climate. This innocent misunderstanding is reflected in much of the language of our culture. Thoughts like, "It scared me stiff," "He made me angry," "Winter depresses me," and "I've got the Monday morning blahs," all imply that emotions are caused by external sources.

Please imagine the following situation. You're in a movie theater watching a movie. Two rows ahead of you a woman stands up, slaps the face of the man sitting next to her, and storms out of the theater. Several people watching nearby have the following emotional responses to this incident. A middle-aged woman feels a tremendous sense of fear. A younger man in the audience has strong feelings of sadness and depression. A teenage girl feels delighted and proud. Another man feels angry and bitter.

What accounts for this diverse array of emotional responses to the exact same event? If the circumstance, a man being slapped by a woman, was the cause, wouldn't it seem logical that the emotional experiences of each observer would be pretty much, if not exactly, the same? Yet, the emotions experienced by these four witnesses were extremely different.

The answer to this riddle is simple when one clearly understands that every human emotion is really people's thoughts in action. The frightened, middle-aged woman had the following thoughts, "Boy, is she in for it now. When he gets home, he's going to beat the heck out of her." She remembered some past incidents when she was physically abused by her ex-husband. The teenage girl, who felt delighted and gleeful, thought, "What an assertive and courageous woman. I wish more women would stand up to men like that." The young man, who felt sad and depressed, thought about his girlfriend walking out on him and said to himself, "He's had it now. She's left him and she'll never come back...he's going to be sad and alone." Finally, the man who felt angry thought, "What a witch. That's just like a woman. He tries his best and she doesn't appreciate it."

Thus, the true source of the very different emotions of each observer was <u>not</u> the event. Rather, each emotion was the product of certain thoughts in each observer's memory coming to mind. The moment we think a thought, we experience an emotion perfectly correlated to it. Our emotions are similar to the soundtrack on each frame of film rotating on the reels of our old friend the movie projector. Emotions are simply another way that we experience our thoughts through our physical senses. Emotions are always the product of our thoughts in action!

Matthew McKay, in his book, *Thoughts and Feelings*, cites several scientific experiments that nicely illustrate this interesting fact of feelings as thought events. One classic experiment involved the administration of adrenaline injections to a subject who was told that the drug was Suproxin, a new vitamin compound. The subject was then placed in an observation room for 15 to 20 minutes. An accomplice of the experimenter, supposedly just Suproxin injected, was brought in to pass the waiting time with the subject. A short while after the adrenaline injection, the subject experienced typical nervous system arousal; hand tremors, heart pounding, and rapid breathing. As the adrenaline took effect, the accomplice began behaving in one of two ways. He either became progressively more angry, or he acted increasingly euphoric and playful.

During this time, the subject was observed through a two-way mirror and his behavior systematically recorded. It was found that those subjects who had waited with the angry accomplice became angry, and those who waited with the euphoric accomplice became euphoric. It was also found that subjects given a salt water placebo had no emotional reaction, no matter how the accomplice functioned. Subjects who were told in advance that Suproxin often had side effects of trembling and heart pounding reported no emotional reaction, regardless of the accomplice's behavior.

The researchers concluded that emotion is not merely a physiological event, a chemical reaction in the body which automatically creates feelings. Physiological arousal, by itself, cannot produce emotions. Emotion is created by people's thoughts about events, both internal (e.g., physiological) and external. Subjects in this study interpreted their physical arousal as either anger or euphoria, depending on what they thought was appropriate, the emotional reaction of the accomplice. If the accomplice was angry, they interpreted the adrenaline reaction as anger, and thereafter expressed and reported feeling angry.

In another classic study, experimental subjects were shown slides of Playboy nudes while supposedly listening to their own heart rates. In fact, they were hearing a recording of random heartbeats that could be altered by the experimenters to speed up or slow down. For half of the slides, subjects heard their "heart rate" increase. These slides were subsequently rated as more attractive than slides for which their heart beat did not change. The experimenters explained their findings by suggesting that subjects convinced themselves that a slide was attractive by actively searching the slide for attributes that might have caused such a dramatic heart rate reaction (i.e., second "the's" that weren't really there)!

Later, these same researchers found that people were more apt to approach a live snake if led to think that their heart rates had not increased while watching the snake. The researchers concluded that an emotional response can depend on what people think their internal state is regardless of what is actually going on inside their body. Once again, thought, activated by consciousness, is the prerequisite for every emotion.

In a final interesting study, the researchers were able to induce angry behavior by merely telling a subject that he or she was angry. Subjects were moderately provoked by two student accomplices. They were then given phony feedback about their emotional response on an "anger meter." The meter was said to measure heart rate, blood pressure, and galvanic skin response or "sweating." Subjects were led to think that they were experiencing either low, medium, or high anger toward their tormentors. The experimenters found a systematic relationship between the anger feedback and electric shocks delivered by the subjects to the students. In other words, the subjects who were led to believe they were more angry administered more shocks to the provoking student. The researchers concluded that subjects looked at the "anger meter," concluded from the readings that they were angry, and then proceeded to feel angry. No actual physiological arousal was necessary...the feeling of anger was entirely dependent on the thought that the emotion was present!

We Always Smell, Taste, and Touch Our Own Thoughts

By the way, you also smell your own thoughts, taste your own thoughts, and even touch your own thoughts in action! Consider the diversity of preferences among people and cultures for food, beverages, aromas, and textures. Why do people in some cultures think that the aroma of body odor is a "turn-on?" Why do men in some cultures like the look and feel of body hair on the legs and underarms of women? Why do some people love the taste of tripe stew, which is made from animal intestines? Why is a termite stir-fry a delicacy in some lands?

Where do you think the terms "learned tastes" or "educated palate" come from? Why do some people devour hot peppers and Tabasco sauce while others can't stand the thought of them? If you went to Puerto Rico and smelled the aroma of mundungo or asepow cooking on a hot stove, would you know what you were smelling? Not until you had learned the thoughts necessary to distinguish these dishes. The bottom line? Every experience of smell, taste and touch is produced by our thoughts in action!

"Reality" is Always Our Next Thought

Let's take a moment to summarize the important distinctions we've considered thus far. First, every bit and morsel of our moment to moment experience of life is produced or generated by our thoughts, hard-wired to our senses, and brought to life by our faculty of consciousness. Of course, every reality illusion that we experience looks real to us in the moment. With low levels of thought recognition, however, people are prone to experience their reality illusions as the "truth," or "absolute realities."

With a shift in understanding about the role that thought plays in their moment to moment experience of life, people instantly recognize that every experience they have is actually a thought event...a momentary reality illusion created by their own thoughts in action. To the degree that people know that they are always forming thought, and that the thoughts they form are translated into apparent realities by their consciousness, they realize that every momentary reality they experience is a fleeting, temporary product of their own mind at work.

That's right...your on-going experience of life is always being created inside of you. You are the movie projector, creating your life on your psychological screen from the inside-out. Your every emotion, perception, smell, taste, touch, and behavior is always a dance perfectly choreographed to the on-going symphony of your thoughts in action. It's not happening to you from the outside-in...it's being created within you from the inside-out. Life's not doing it to you from out there. You've never, ever been at the effect of your circumstances...just your thoughts. As human beings, what we call "reality," is always our next thought.

Imagine that you wrote yourself some threatening notes, forgot that you wrote them, found them later, read them, and scared yourself to death! That's how life tends to appear to people when they have a low level of thought recognition. Like a dog chasing its tail, not realizing that it's attached to his own body, when people don't understand the principles of mind, consciousness, and thought, they often chase after life as if it's really happening to them from the outside-in. Now you can see why thought recognition is a major key to residing in the neighborhood of List A.

Thought Reconditioning Isn't the Answer

At this point, some of you may be wondering, "Now I realize that my experience of life is created moment to moment from the inside-out through my thoughts in action. Now I'm clear that my on-going life experience is always being generated from within me. Now that I have these understandings, how can I start using them to spend more time in the neighborhood of List A? Should I start uncovering, challenging and refuting my dysfunctional thoughts? Should I work at perfecting the art of positive thinking? Should I practice cognitive restructuring or thought stopping? What about learning positive affirmations and guided imagery?"

It's interesting that so many people think that the way to higher levels of mental health is through diligently working to change the content or quality of their thoughts. In fact, many contemporary psychotherapeutic models support this misguided idea. For years, I taught people how to use scores of tools and techniques to actively alter and recondition their dysfunctional thoughts and beliefs. I encouraged people to actively fight their irrational thoughts, and challenge their distorted ideas. At the time, I didn't realize that these strategies were actually symptoms of mental dysfunction rather than ways to achieve genuine mental health.

The true answer to residing primarily in the neighborhood of List A is not by actively challenging, refuting, or altering the content of any of your thoughts. In fact, to live in List A, you don't have to do a lick of work at changing your thoughts. You don't have to uncover and refute any so-called "dysfunctional" beliefs. You don't have to use one iota of positive thinking. There's absolutely no need for positive imagery or affirmation habits!

All of these techniques and tools of thought content manipulation represent another variation of the misguided "more, better, different" game that we visited earlier. This version goes something like this. People will be happier if they actively work at thinking _more_ positive thoughts, or if they get _better_ at avoiding negative thoughts, or if they actively force themselves to think about things in a _different_ way.

Actively working to change your thought content can never lead you back to your birthright. Deliberately changing your thoughts can never bring you to the realization that your divine gift of thought was designed to function in a healthy way <u>totally on its own</u>...a way that <u>naturally and effortlessly</u> produces a wise, intelligent, responsive stream of thought. When your divine gift of thought is free to operate in this innate, healthy way, more rich and fulfilling List A moments will <u>automatically and effortlessly</u> be yours.

Recognizing the Natural Design of Your Two Thinking Modes

A breakthrough in understanding about the principle of Thought is a major key to taking up residence in the neighborhood of List A. There is, however, a second key shift in understanding that's even more essential to releasing your birthright of healthy psychological functioning. This understanding shift has to do with the innate, natural way that your divine gift of thought was meant to operate most of the time.

In Chapter Four, you finally discovered your true identity. You realized that who you truly are is a human being with the gift of thought. That wasn't the whole story, however. If you recall, there was a second part to your true self...your gift of thought came with a natural built in design to operate in a high quality way without any conscious effort from you!

It's very helpful for people to clearly distinguish the effortless, passive way they were designed to think most of the time. It's also essential that people realize how to effectively use the active, more effortful way they learned to think. Why? **Because the quality of our life experience in each and every moment is directly linked to the efficient operation of our two modes of thinking**. Once you've experienced this second breakthrough in understanding, you will finally realize how to regularly access the one and only true source of effortless happiness and inner peace. How good can you stand it!

Chapter 8

Distinguishing Your **Two** Modes of Thinking

Please try to remember a time in your life when you were totally absorbed or lost in some event or activity. It might have been a sport or a game that you were playing. It could have been your hobby or a work assignment. Perhaps it was a time at the beach, lounging in the sun. Maybe you were hiking in the woods on a beautiful autumn day. Whatever you were doing, it was a time when your thinking was so quiet, so effortless, that it was virtually invisible. While it may have felt like there was nothing on your mind, you were actually immersed in an intelligent, responsive stream of thought. These useful thoughts just glided by, one quiet thought after another.

You didn't have to deliberately think about what you were doing. The exact thoughts you needed just came to you, seemingly from "out of the blue." Useful memories were effortlessly retrieved and processed. Fresh, creative thoughts and original ideas seemed to appear out of nowhere. Virtually every thought necessary to carry out your activity just occurred to you in the moment.

Naturally and intuitively, you recalled and utilized every memory, every skill, and every ability you needed, exactly when you needed them. Helpful thoughts, responsive to the moment, just glided by in an orderly, wise, productive flow.

It's likely that your perspective of time was altered. Hours may have passed and seemed like minutes. You responded in perfect harmony with what each moment required. You felt virtually no stress nor tension, no self-consciousness nor concern about your performance. It was an extremely fulfilling, satisfying, enlivening, even exhilarating experience. If such an event was rare for you, you may have thought of it as a peak experience, even a spiritual one!

Have you ever had this kind of experience? Some people have them on a regular basis. Most people have at least one area of their life that they do naturally, where they're "in the groove," without worry or second thoughts about what they're doing. In these areas, people seem to "know" what to do without thinking. Judy Sedgeman, a faculty member with the Psychology of Mind Training Institute, describes it this way:

> "A businessman might anticipate the market and always make a right decision at the ideal moment, or an athlete might take advantage of every split second of opportunity on the field, or an actor might become totally believable to his audience in every role, or a musician might perform at levels that seem to transcend the limits of her instrument or her voice. If asked to describe their level of effort, they would be confused by the question. They might honestly say they didn't really find their work effortful; it just seemed obvious to them or it came readily, or it was a 'gift'."

These wondrous, high quality moments of life are the ones we all savor and cherish. They're extremely rich and satisfying. Just what is the source of these exhilarating, fulfilling times? Why don't we have them more often? Wouldn't it be great if we could access them on a regular basis? What if they were available to each of us as a way of life?

Free-Flowing Thinking: The Natural Way You Were Born To Think

Please get ready for some great news. These wonderful, List A experiences of high quality psychological functioning <u>are</u> available to us in each and every moment. They're not created by positive thinking, rational thinking, or any other thought reconditioning ritual. Their source is always the same...a natural, intelligent, high-quality kind of thinking. This thinking mode is our generic human thought process...the effortless, responsive, lucid way the human mind was designed to think most of the time. This innate, natural thinking process effortlessly and automatically produces high quality, List A psychological experiences. Psychology of Mind calls this intelligent, generic thinking process, **Mode One - Free-Flowing Thinking**.

Please take a moment and recall some times in your life when you felt genuinely satisfied, fulfilled, and content. Please reflect on those times when you felt graceful, spontaneous, and very much at ease. Times when you were totally un-self-conscious, when you went with the flow and interacted with life in perfect harmony. During those high quality moments, were you deliberately thinking? During those rich, full moments, were you consciously aware of any thinking going on? It's likely that you weren't. Why? Because during those high quality times, your mind was thinking effortlessly, in its natural, free-flowing, passive way. This innate, healthy thinking mode was automatically generating an intelligent responsive flow of thought that produced your easy, graceful, exhilarating experience of living.

Accessing Your Free-Flowing Thinking

Accessing high quality, free-flowing thinking is actually quite simple. You see, free-flowing thinking automatically kicks in as soon as we quiet or clear our mind. Whenever we suspend our deliberate or intentional thinking, free-flowing thinking immediately fills the vacuum. Instantly, an intelligent, responsive stream of thought begins flowing freely through our mind in a gentle, relaxed way.

Whenever we stop deliberately trying to figure out or analyze life, we free our mind to think in this natural, quiet way. Once our mind is clear, it begins to operate like a receiver or channel through which an intelligent stream of fresh, original thoughts and useful memories can quietly flow. Joe Bailey, in his new POM book, *Slowing Down to the Speed of Life*, talks about accessing free-flowing thinking:

> "To gain access to free-flowing thought we must first know that it exists, and we must value the power of it. Second, we must have faith that if we clear the mind (let go of our analytical thinking), this mode will automatically start feeding us a flow of thoughts - which it will...Clearing the mind is much like letting the silt settle in water. You simply do nothing and the silt automatically settles. Anything you do to try to settle the silt actually keeps it stirred up...By letting go of the analytical, trying-to-figure-it-out mode, we create a vacuum that the free-flowing mode will fill."

Mode One - free flowing thinking is the effortless, high quality thinking process that people universally describe as relaxing, fresh, insightful, intuitive, and creative. This natural, health-generating thought mode is your human birthright. In fact, a human being designed to think primarily in an effortless, free-flowing way is who you truly are. You didn't have to learn to think in the free-flowing mode. You were born with the gift of thought already designed to operate in this natural, high quality way most of the time.

As soon as we access our free-flowing thinking, we automatically begin responding in harmony with life as it comes at us point blank in each moment. When we quiet our mind and ease into the intelligent, gliding stream of thought, our thinking instantly matches the speed of life. That's why we feel so present and absorbed in the moment. That's why we're able to respond to each wake and swirl of life with more balance and flexibility. As a champion rodeo rider moves with the undulations of a bucking bronco, or an Olympic kayaker responds to the surging rapids of a white water course, free-flowing thinking enables us to move gracefully with the waves and currents of our life without effort or stress.

The minds of very young children operate predominantly in the free-flowing mode. That's why children live fully in the moment...spend more time "in the zone"...really taste the ice cream...feel the water...smell the flowers...become their imaginings...burst with love...anticipate with passion...and express themselves with incredible spontaneity and enthusiasm. That's why these children typically experience a group of deeper human feelings. An infant, for example, doesn't have to learn to laugh or feel joyful. Young children are easily, if not unconditionally, contented. When placed with another person in pain, they have natural feelings of compassion. They experience no self-consciousness, and therefore, have a natural humility and self-esteem.

The Natural Intelligence of Free-Flowing Thinking

There is a powerful intelligence inherent in free-flowing thinking which gives people wiser perspectives and has them see more responsive and appropriate behaviors in each moment. In his book, *The Renaissance of Psychology*, Dr. George Pransky, co-founder of Psychology of Mind, describes this natural intelligence:

> "Free-flowing thinking is always responsive to the present moment...responsiveness ranges from the day to day practical to the sublime. A hungry person in the free-flowing mode will notice restaurants along the highway. A tired person will notice hotels. A person facing difficulties in this mode will have insights that are ideal solutions to the problems that have baffled him. Forgotten appointments will come to mind through this mode. We noticed in our

private practice, for example, that stressed-out businessmen who were pushing themselves and were sleep-deprived would instantly fall asleep as soon as their minds were free and clear. The free-flowing mode thinking was protecting them from their own devices."

The more people understand the natural power of free-flowing thinking, the more they begin to trust it, quiet their mind, and ease into it. Depending on how quiet our mind becomes, we can experience infinite levels or depths of the free-flowing mode. At each level, the power of this incredible thinking increases. At any depth, we always access a natural intelligence, mental clarity, common sense, and desirable feelings. In quieter states of mind, we get insights and intuitive understanding about life that we haven't even anticipated...profound awareness that can change our life. At its deepest level, Mode One is the thinking mode of genius and creativity...the mode from which all historic ideas and scientific breakthroughs have emerged.

Free-flowing thinking can access all of the thoughts stored in our memory. It can call upon all the information, ideas, and thoughts that we already know. What's truly amazing, however, is that this thinking mode can also access ideas and thoughts from the unknown, or what we don't consciously realize that we "know." Put another way, there is also a transcendent intelligence in Mode One. Free-flowing thinking has the ability to access a creative, intelligent stream of fresh, original thought that precedes our memory. George Pransky eloquently describes the transcendent intelligence of free-flowing thinking:

"When we observed the operation of Mode One - free-flowing thinking in ourselves and our clients, we were struck by the intelligence and responsiveness of this mode. We noticed that this mode gave people ideas that were clearly beyond the capabilities of their own learning and experience. Children display wisdom beyond their years. People like Albert Einstein come up with theories beyond their education that must be analyzed and proven by people with much more education and expertise than themselves. We've all had the experience of coming up with ideas and thinking to ourselves, 'I'm amazed that I could come up with an idea like that.' Writers and musicians will admit puzzlement about the quality of their creations, admitting that their products are way beyond their education and their known level of expertise. There is obviously a transcendent intelligence behind Mode One that cnables us to come up with original ideas and that enables us to have thoughts that are beyond our memories, our experience, and our education."

Thinking primarily in the free-flowing mode is how all of us were designed to think. You didn't have to learn to think in this high quality way anymore than you had to learn how to breathe correctly or to use your heart or kidneys in the right way. When you're thinking in Mode One, you don't notice it any more than you notice your lungs breathing, or your heart pumping. Each of these innate human functions was designed to operate invisibly and effortlessly in the background, naturally producing it's respective experience of health. Mode One - free-flowing thinking is the one and only source of effortless happiness and inner peace. Free-flowing thinking is your automatic pilot to List A!

Processing Thinking: The Active "Effortful" Way You Learned to Think

There's a second mode of thinking that's also available to all human beings. This way of thinking needs absolutely no introduction. Why? Because this thinking mode is, without a doubt, the preeminent way of thinking in our culture today. Most people have come to see this type of thinking as "normal" thinking...perhaps even the only mode of thinking available to them. Most of us have learned to use this thinking mode most of the time. Psychology of Mind calls this learned way of thinking, **Mode Two - Processing Thinking**.

Pretty impressive, right? Well, you might want to hold your applause for a moment until I tell you a little bit more. Processing thinking is the thinking mode that's primarily responsible for the present condition of our country's public education system, our political system, our justice system, and our international relations. It's also the thinking mode that's mainly responsible for the typical quality of our marital and family relationships, race relations, job satisfaction, and our popular media products. Furthermore, this thinking mode is the <u>sole</u> source of all of the stress, unhappiness, and discontent on the entire planet!

Not as much to cheer about as you might have first thought. Let me quickly reassure you, however. Mode Two - processing thinking is actually a very helpful thinking mode. It has not only provided a useful service to humanity since the beginning of time, it's an absolute necessity for all of us. Unfortunately, this very useful thinking process has been horribly abused. While it still serves us in some very helpful ways, most of us have innocently learned to chronically overuse and misuse it. By so doing, we have inadvertently turned it into a monster. For most of us, artificial processing thinking has replaced the natural free-flowing mode as the master of our thinking.

In Chapter Nine, we'll examine in detail how we innocently learned to abuse this essential thinking mode. For the time being, however, let's step back and pay this useful thinking process its due respect. Let's distinguish Mode Two - processing thinking from Mode One - free-flowing thinking, and get crystal clear about how each mode was meant to be used. This is perhaps the most useful understanding breakthrough available on our journey. Why? **Because the quality of our life experience in each and every moment is a function of using our two modes of thinking in the precise way they were designed to be used!**

Comparing Thinking Modes One and Two

Mode One - free-flowing thinking and Mode Two - processing thinking are as different as night and day. For one thing, the free-flowing thinking is the generic, natural thinking process that was our gift at birth. Free-flowing thinking is our psychological immune system...it's natural job is to keep us living in the moment in a full, rich way. Processing thinking, on the other hand, is an artificial way of thinking that we all had to learn to use. We were taught to think in the processing mode...to use our mind like a computer to actively process, analyze, and deliberately think about things. The job of processing thinking is to store useful thoughts in our memory and to process them when it makes sense to do so. Like inhaling and exhaling, we're either thinking in Mode One or Mode Two. It's impossible to do both at the same time.

Like any natural process, such as breathing or swallowing, free-flowing thinking is effortless. There is no stress factor in this natural thinking mode. Processing thinking, on the other hand, always requires a certain amount of concentration, effort, or stress. Since it takes effort, processing thinking is always noticeable. Because of the stress factor built into this mode, young children initially resist it. At first it's often difficult to get them to sit down, actively focus, and use processing thinking to learn things like how to tell time or tie shoelaces. Because thinking in Mode Two takes children out of their effortless flowing thinking, they initially experience it as foreign or unnatural.

Free-flowing thinking always produces a natural movement or flow of thoughts through our mind. This thought flow occurs automatically unless, and until, we deliberately intervene and start actively "squeezing" or holding our thoughts in place. In the free-flowing mode, responsive thoughts naturally form and dissolve, form and dissolve in our mind over and over again in a continuous process. The essence of free-flowing thinking is the fact that thoughts naturally pass through our mind instead of being held in place and deliberately processed.

In the processing mode, on the other hand, we actively pull thoughts from our memory and deliberately think about them or hold them in place in our mind. In processing thinking, our natural free-flow thinking stops while we entertain, hold onto, or re-think certain thoughts over and over again. In the processing mode we always allow thoughts to stagnate or remain stuck in our mind.

Finally, the free-flowing mode allows us to access creative ideas and insights from our transcendent human intelligence...fresh, original thoughts that are not available in our memory. Mode One is not limited, it can access the known as well as the unknown. Data from our memory as well as original ideas can come through free-flowing thinking. The processing mode, on the other hand, always limits us to looking for ideas or solutions within the confines of our already-existing knowledge or memories. Thus, the realities produced by Mode Two are always predictable and redundant.

Useful Processing Thinking

Like I said earlier, there's nothing inherently wrong with Mode Two - processing thinking. When it's used appropriately, the processing mode is indispensable for a variety of important tasks. For example, Mode Two is essentially the mode of choice for many types of analysis. When people calculate the amount of material necessary to sew a dress, or figure out the details for an upcoming wedding reception, or decide on the appropriate time to leave for the airport, they bring to mind the necessary information, actively process it, and arrive at specific conclusions.

Thus, processing thinking is always very useful for things like logistics, financial calculations, and comparisons...for anything where a known formula is applied to specific known variables.

Also, the processing mode is essential for linking useful thoughts together and assigning them to memory. George Pransky cites one example of using processing thinking for such useful programming:

"...When people make left turns in a car, for example, they go through a complex and intricate learned procedure: they look in the rear view mirror, put on the turn signal, move out to the left, move to a certain place in the intersection, look in both directions, and make the turn. New drivers attempting such a turn struggle to pay attention to and process every move when they first get behind the wheel of a car."

Eventually, this useful Mode Two learning gets programmed into memory so that when the situation presents itself (e.g., turning left), the thought chain is triggered and we automatically carry out the task. At that point, learning that we've acquired essentially in Mode Two can be utilized effortlessly in Mode One. Most everyone, for example, has had the experience of intuitively driving a car, effortlessly performing calculations, or without thinking, recalling the appropriate information to solve a particular problem. This is our natural Mode One - free-flowing thinking at work, effortlessly utilizing the learning we've initially done in Mode Two - processing thinking.

Most of the thought programs that we've assigned to memory are very useful, even essential for effectively playing the game of life in our culture. For example, essential abilities like reading, writing, and doing math all require thought habits acquired through the processing mode. Complex skills like driving an automobile, hitting a golf ball, repairing an engine, and doing nuclear physics, likewise depend on the linking together of hundreds of thoughts in our memory.

When you consider the advantages of having such thought chains in our memory, it's hard to imagine living effectively without them. If we didn't have such programming, then every day we'd have to relearn basic things like how to dress ourselves, how to make breakfast, how to drive our car, and how to find our way to work! Without these helpful processing mode habits of thinking, every minute would be filled with countless decisions that we would have to deliberate over and over again.

Free-Flowing Thinking the Master - Processing Thinking Our Helpful Servant

At this point, you may be wondering, "If the overall quality of my experience of life is determined by keeping my mind clear and trusting my natural free-flowing thinking to guide me...and yet, processing thinking is also essential...how can I use both in the most efficient way?" Good question, and there's a very specific answer. Here's how it works. First of all, our natural human design is for Mode One - free-flowing thinking to be the master or director of our thinking. When the free-flowing mode is at the helm, it will always prompt us whenever it's wise and makes sense to move into Mode Two - processing thinking. Our natural, free-flowing thinking can access either the intelligent stream of original, insightful thoughts that precedes our memory or prompt us to shift into Mode Two and deliberately process the thoughts or information in our memory when it's appropriate to do so.

In the free-flowing mode, if life requests a response from us where processing thinking makes sense, we will be quietly nudged by an intelligent thought to shift into Mode Two. When our thinking is free-flowing, our shifts into processing thinking will always be useful and appropriate. Mode Two - processing thinking was always meant to be used at the wise discretion of our natural, flowing thinking. We weren't meant to have to deliberately, or effortfully analyze, or figure out how to respond to life. Our lives were meant to unfold spontaneously under the wise direction of flowing thinking. When we trust our mind to think in its natural free-flowing way, processing thinking always acts as our faithful servant, making our lives more effective and productive. George Pransky puts it this way:

> "As people learn, in essence, to leave their thinking alone--that is, to let Mode One - free-flowing thinking guide them in and out of Mode Two - processing thinking as needed and to refrain from grabbing onto any thought and deliberately processing it, their thinking is increasingly fruitful, productive, wise, and common-sense, regardless of whether it is memory or original thinking."

Here's a personal example of the healthy interplay between these two thinking modes. While writing this book, I would clear my mind and move into free flowing thinking as often as possible. Thus, my typical experience of writing over the past two years was effortless, exhilarating, and spontaneous. Ideas and examples would just pop into my head. Just the right words and phrases were at my fingertips. Useful thoughts flowed effortlessly through my mind, often faster than I could write. If a less useful, even negative thought floated by, I had the perspective to see it for what it was, and to let it go.

Sometimes it felt like I was a receiver or channel through which my thoughts were effortlessly flowing. Often, memories came to mind in fresh, creative ways. I had no awareness of retrieving or processing them...they just showed up and got processed naturally. Hours would pass and often it seemed like minutes. Later I was often amazed at the vast number of helpful memories and insightful ideas I'd spontaneously seen and effortlessly utilized.

Occasionally, as I was writing in Mode One, I got prompted by an intelligent thought that told me to "bone up" on a particular POM principle or distinction. Then, I would shift into Mode Two, and start deliberately focusing on certain information. While this processing experience was more effortful, it was always necessary and appropriate to the goal of my writing. If I kept processing for too long, I usually got another intelligent thought to take a rest, clear my mind, and move back into Mode One.

Also, when we allow the free-flowing mode to direct our thinking, it provides us with wise, intuitive thoughts necessary to distinguish useful memories from other, more biased, less functional ones. It supplies us with the insightful thoughts needed to see our less productive thought programs for what they really are. It gives us the wisdom and perspective to avoid squeezing or re-thinking less useful memories and to let them float by. For example, a person could have thoughts of "killing a stranger" come and go through his mind in the free-flowing mode and such thoughts wouldn't be problematic. It would look to that person like some of those random, crazy thoughts that people sometimes have. Instantly, he would dismiss them. Thus, the distinguishing quality of Mode One is not the particular content of the thoughts that pass through it, but rather the <u>fact that thoughts pass through and keep flowing freely</u>.

Please think about it. Recall a time when your mind was thinking quietly in the free-flowing mode. How did you experience your memories coming to mind? Did you have to deliberately recall and effortfully process them, or did they tend to show up spontaneously and get processed with virtually no effort? Were these memories mostly biased and unproductive, or useful and responsive to the situation at hand? If a painful or weird one happened to sneak in, was it difficult or easy to view it with perspective and to let it float by?

The Quality of Our Present Moments

When you think about it, the present is all that we ever have. The quality of our life is literally the quality of our on-going present moments. What determines the richness of our successive moments of now? That's right...it's the quality of our thinking. What's the highest quality thinking possible? You've got it...the highest quality thinking occurs when we allow the free-flowing mode to guide us. Thinking primarily in the free-flowing mode is the one and only source of rich, satisfying, and fulfilling List A present moments. Living life in the free-flowing stream of intelligent, responsive thought, naturally produces full, rich, List A moments of now.

Free-flowing thinking always creates a much higher quality experience of the present than that produced by deliberately or indiscriminately processing our memories. Allan Flood, author of the wonderful POM book, *The Perfect Misfortune*, puts it this way:

"You and I live in the moment - we have no choice about that. We can live in the moment bound by a reality spawned from our memories (beliefs, opinions, judgments, values), or we can live in the moment created by the wonder of the natural, constantly flowing stream of thought that precedes our memories. Living in that flowing stream of natural, responsive, gliding thought gives us the life we want - fulfilling, satisfying. Anything that takes us out of that stream gives us headaches (physical and emotional)."

Living a life generated by the chronic, deliberate processing of our memories is effortful, redundant, stultifying, and often painful. Why? Because when we're experiencing life through our memories in action, we can only see more, better, or different variations of what we already know. Viewing life through our memories always limits us to the redundant, predictable feelings, perceptions, and behaviors spawned by our already-existing beliefs, opinions, judgments, and points of view. Experiencing life primarily in this way would be like driving an automobile, misguidedly looking ahead through the rear view mirror, instead of the windshield. You might think you were seeing the future fresh and new. Actually, you'd always be seeing more of the past.

Here's another way to look at it. Imagine that your life is like a two-drawer file cabinet. The top drawer is meant for the present and the bottom drawer for the past. Experiencing life through the deliberate processing of your memories would be like misfiling your past files in your present drawer. By so doing, you'd have little or no room in the present to experience life in fresh, new ways. When people recognize, trust, and ease into free-flowing thinking, their past files are instantly transported to the proper drawer. When it makes sense, one gets pulled quietly into the present and usefully processed. When our thinking is free-flowing, our memories can't contaminate our natural ability to experience our present moments in fresh, rich, spontaneous ways.

Please let me share another personal example. My experience of teaching at the University used to come primarily from the deliberate processing of the knowledge in my memory, not from the stream. In other words, semester after semester, I would come to class, and deliberately lecture using the processing mode. I would put my notes on the lectern, and pretty much say the same old things, tell the same old stories, and ask the same old questions. I could put on a pretty good show, and was considered by most students to be a competent teacher. Yet, the truth be known, my lectures were redundant and predictable. They were seldom inspiring because I seldom felt inspired. It was rare that they would come alive in a passionate or exhilarating way.

Now, when I teach my classes, I quiet my mind. I avoid deliberately processing my memories. I do my best to allow my natural, intelligent, flowing thinking to come alive. I still bring my notes and my memories with me, of course. However, they no longer serve as the master or director of my lecturing. Now, I simply trust my natural, intelligent, flowing thinking to kick in and show me the way.

The experience of lecturing from the stream is often exhilarating. Helpful thoughts just flow into my mind. I have no conscious awareness of thinking them. Sometimes, if appropriate, they direct me to my notes. Other times they inspire me to do, try, and say things in fresh, creative ways. Please don't get me wrong, my lectures are still orderly and clear. They make sense and are on target. They're simply more spontaneous, more heartfelt, more passionate, and tied more to my vision of what's possible in my field of study. Also, when I lecture from the stream, my students are more present and engaged than ever before.

I used to be asleep when I taught. The experience of deliberately speaking through the knowledge in my memory was predictable, redundant, and at times, downright boring. Now, I feel more awake and alive in my classes. Each session is an adventure in which I'm carried to new experiences and fresh perspectives by staying in the stream of intelligent, responsive, gliding thought.

What if it All Stopped Here? Experiencing Life From the Stream

What would our typical experience of life be like if it all stopped here? What would our usual experience of life be like if we thought predominantly in Mode One - free-flowing thinking? As the master or director of our thinking, the free-flowing mode could access the fresh, wise, insightful stream of original thought, or prompt us to process our memories for useful purposes. It's helpful to see that if we trusted the free-flowing mode to direct our thinking, we would automatically experience most of our present moments in more fulfilling, satisfying, and enlivening ways. We would automatically live in the neighborhood of List A most of the time.

If we typically trusted the stream to guide us, we would naturally experience clarity, perspective, common sense, intuition, and wisdom. We would access deeper human feelings like contentment, happiness, inspiration, compassion, and peace of mind. We would experience a natural self-esteem. Coping with life would be the rare exception, not the rule. We would typically behave in more intelligent, mature, productive, common sense ways. Best of all...each of these wonderful, List A experiences would take no conscious effort or struggle. Our gift of free-flowing thinking is the one and only true source of effortless happiness and inner peace.

Now, here's some more great news. Your mind is as healthy now as it was when you were born. It hasn't been damaged, it hasn't worn out, and it certainly hasn't forgotten its natural design to think primarily in a free-flowing way. At this very moment, your mind is ready and waiting to operate in sync with its natural design principles. Within you, right now, is a mother lode of psychological health just waiting to be released. During those times you already spend in the neighborhood of List A, your mind is simply doing its natural, healthy thing...thinking quietly in the free-flowing mode! Free-flowing thinking is available to all of us, in each and every moment. Dr. George Pransky eloquently summarizes the profound utility of this incredible, virtually untapped human resource:

> "To repeat and emphasize the central point: Psychology of Mind suggests that Mode One - free-flowing thinking is available to all people, always, <u>as a way of life</u>. Mode One is a birthright. This mode provides the feelings that people want for themselves. It provides a transcendent intelligence for problem-solving. It provides a clear mind so that people can have an uncontaminated view of life to

enjoy the moment. It even provides us with prompts about when to use Mode Two - processing thinking. Mode One is free from chronic stress and distress. It enables our humanity to come through in our personal relationships.   Mode One - free-flowing thinking is the most undiscovered and unappreciated resource in human existence."

Please consider the following questions. Is the free-flowing mode the primary master or director of your thinking? Do you think in a quiet, free-flowing way most of the time? If your answer is no, or you think there's some room for improvement, it's likely that you've innocently learned to abuse Mode Two - processing thinking.   By so doing, you began to short-circuit the natural, healthy operation of your birthright of free-flowing thought. **The abuse of processing thinking is the mental health contaminator.** By recognizing how you innocently learned to abuse this useful, learned thinking ability, you can stop doing so, and start living in the stream as a way of life. How good can you stand it!

Chapter 9

Abusing the "Processing Mode" - The Mental Health Contaminator

N ow you've had another key shift in understanding. Now you realize the one and only true source of high quality psychological functioning. The only way to reside in List A as a way of life, is to allow your natural free-flowing thinking to guide you.

Everything we do in life is more rich and full under the masterful guidance of the natural, responsive stream of free-flowing thought. "Bathing in the stream" makes any activity, from balancing a checkbook or washing the dishes, to doing brain surgery or climbing a mountain, more fulfilling and satisfying. When we start experiencing any aspect of our life as stressful or a "problem" (e.g., our job, marriage, self-worth), it simply means that we've started deliberately thinking in a lower quality way that's taken us out of the stream. Free-flowing thinking is the natural human source of effortless happiness and inner peace!

Also, you now know that there's a second thinking mode, a learned way of thinking that's always noticeable because it takes conscious effort. Mode Two - processing thinking involves the deliberate processing of information or personal knowledge stored in one's memory. In this acquired, artificial thinking mode, people deliberately retrieve thoughts from their memory, hold them in place, and re-think them. Processing thinking is very useful for things like logistics, financial calculations, and comparisons. It's an essential thinking tool for many types of learning and analysis. Mode Two thinking is always, and only, useful when applying a known formula to specific known variables (e.g., reading a road map).

Now you're clear that processing thinking was always meant to be used under the wise direction of the free-flowing mode. When we simply leave our thinking alone, and allow our flowing thinking to guide us in and out of processing thinking as needed, we're always List A fine. It's only when we actively intervene, indiscriminately grab onto our thoughts, hold them in place, and deliberately process them that we're likely to find List B trouble!

Learning to Abuse the Processing Mode

The other day, I decided to observe some pre-school children at my girlfriend Penny's daycare center. For about two hours I risked being in the same room with about twelve healthy children between the ages of two and four. The first thing I noticed was pretty obvious. Most of the time, these children were fully present in the moment. They were completely absorbed in their play and other learning activities. They were curious, involved, spontaneous, and very self-expressive.

Very soon, however, something else became evident. Every now and then, the state of mind of one child or another would suddenly shift. For example, Jimmy became angry and snatched a toy from his playmate. Little Susie suddenly started crying and ran to a teacher. Robbie stomped off into a corner and sulked. Suddenly, Brandon started showing off by knocking down a Lego sculpture. Another child abruptly stopped what she was doing and looked sad and forlorn.

These sudden mood shifts happened periodically throughout my entire observation. While they took several behavioral forms, they all had certain things in common. First, they were very short-lived. Each episode lasted from a few seconds to perhaps a few minutes. Second, once they were over they were over. They seemed to end as abruptly as they began. Once they were complete, each child moved back into healthy gear, becoming fully engaged in his activities once again as if nothing had ever happened!

What accounts for this common phenomenon in healthy youngsters? They seem to live in the neighborhood of List A most of the time. Yet, on occasion, they quickly, often dramatically, move into List B. Then, after very short visits, they spring back into List A as if their List B detours had never occurred.

Please consider the following explanation. Most of the time, the thinking of healthy children is free-flowing. Thus, most of the time these children experience life from the stream, and effortlessly reside in the community of List A. Every now and then, however, the quality of their thinking changes, often dramatically. Every so often, even the healthiest children start thinking in a lower quality way. They misguidedly start re-thinking the same thoughts over and over again in rapid succession. By so doing, they override or short-circuit their natural, free-flowing thinking, and move temporarily into List B.

Take Susie, for example, the little girl at the daycare center who started crying and ran to her teacher. Susie started holding her thoughts in place and blocking her free-flowing thinking. The thought that Susie kept squeezing was, "Billy pinched me." Sobbing profusely, she must have said this to her teacher at least ten times, "Billy pinched me"..."Billy pinched me." Susie tenaciously held onto this thought, allowing this "painful" memory to stagnate in her mind, and generate some painful, List B experiences.

Susie, however, like all healthy children, hadn't yet learned to override her free-flowing thinking like a habit. Thus, with a little TLC, a distraction of some sort, the simple passage of a little time, or the observation of something going on in another part of the room, Susie was quick to let go of her "painful" thoughts. Instantly, her thinking started flowing freely, and she was back in the List A stream once again!

For very young children, such lower quality thinking episodes are like summer thunderstorms. They happen occasionally, they're part of their natural human psychological weather, they're usually quite brief, followed by the sunshine of free-flowing thinking, and quickly forgotten.

I left Penny's daycare center that day realizing how different life would be for most of us adults if we had continued to relate to our lower quality thinking episodes in the same way we once did as very young children. I saw how our typical time spent experiencing life outside the stream would be much shorter indeed. During our lower quality thinking storms, we would be much less likely to continue squeezing our memories, painful or otherwise, for very long. Thus, the likelihood of our becoming gripped by them, stewing in pain, and acting in foolish ways would be substantially reduced. Much sooner, we'd be back in the stream, basking in the warm List A sun!

What happened? How did so many of us lose the natural, wisdom about our lower quality thinking episodes that we once had as children? Why now, when the quality of our thinking drops, do so many of us persist in squeezing our often "painful" memories and short-circuiting our free-flowing thinking for hours, days, months, even years? Why on earth would we do this when it so often means giving up our satisfying home in List A, and moving lock, stock and barrel into the highs and turmoil of List B?

Please consider the possibility that as we grew up, most of us innocently learned to seriously abuse Mode Two - processing thinking. Along the way, most of us misguidedly learned, practiced, and may have even perfected several lower quality processing mode thinking habits.

The following case example nicely illustrates this unfortunate learning process. It concerns a very nice family that I counseled a few years ago. Johnny, age six, was basically a happy child. He was outgoing, sociable, playful, very kind, and considerate. His mother, a very caring person, was also the quintessential worrier. One day little Johnny came home from school looking very sad. His mother, feeling quite stressed that day, over-reacted. With an anxious look on her face, she rushed over to Johnny and urgently asked him what was wrong. Johnny, startled by his mother's reaction, began to cry. To this, his mother became even more anxious and started screaming, "What's wrong?...What's wrong?" Johnny, really upset at this point, began crying even louder. His mother frantically grabbed the telephone and called her husband at work. Their conversation, which Johnny overheard, went something like this, "Jim (sobbing)...you've got to come home. Something's happened to Johnny. Yes, he's here. No, he's not hurt. But he's horribly upset, and I just know that someone at that school may have touched him or something. No, I can't get him to talk about it because he won't stop crying. Okay...well, please come home as soon as you can!"

For the rest of the afternoon, Johnny and his mother went over every minute of his day at school. Johnny told her that he didn't know why he was so sad. His mother, however, convinced that something bad must have happened to him, continued to grill him about the day's events. Later that day when his father arrived, both parents continued to question Johnny, who by then was enrolled in the "something bad must have occurred" theory.

That night, Johnny had a nightmare and woke up crying and shaking. Both parents rushed to his room and while nervously comforting him, again began analyzing the possible explanations for their son's "unusual" behavior. They decided that the only thing to do was take him to see a psychologist. Johnny finally fell asleep and his parents went back to bed feeling anxious and depressed.

The following morning, Johnny awakened complaining of a headache and pleading to stay home from school.

To make a long story short, nothing bad happened to Johnny. He just had a lower quality processing thinking episode. In other words, some "sad" thoughts came down the stream and Johnny started holding them in place and squeezing them. Startled by the emotional reaction of his mother, Johnny added some additional frightening thoughts to his processing mode thought dam. By the time they brought him to see me, he had developed a severe case of what psychologists call separation anxiety, and a school phobia as well!

What started out as a simple mood swing, a temporary episode of lower quality processing thinking, which, if left alone, would have quickly run its course, turned into a processing mode thinking habit called "worrying." Johnny's dependent and phobic behaviors were the best way that he could see to cope with his processing mode-activated, anxious feelings. Innocently, Johnny's parents were teaching him to chronically misuse Mode Two and live outside of the stream.

Processing Mode Abuse #1 - Overuse

There are two ways in which processing thinking can be abused...by overusing it and misusing it. The overuse and misuse of this helpful thinking mode is the source of every ounce of human stress and unhappiness. Let's start by examining the overuse of Mode Two. If you recall, processing thinking always takes effort. Therefore, even if it's used for useful purposes, because of the stress factor in this mode, chronic processing thinking will result in stress or even mental burnout. George Pransky describes the result of overusing processing thinking or having a "busy mind:"

> "...Even if it is used properly, people who do too much Mode Two - processing thinking experience fatigue, exaggerated mood swings, and excessive emotionality. To overuse the processing mode would be equivalent to abusing the body with sleep

deprivation and expending energy beyond a person's own tolerances. People who have overactive minds through excessive use of the processing mode experience boredom and stress."

I used to do hours on end of psychotherapy with processing thinking typically at the helm. First, I learned one of the two hundred psychotherapy models available at the time. I gathered as much information as I could about this model from books, classes, and seminars. With all this information stored away in my memory, I finally began working with people. Instead of trusting my free-flowing thinking to guide me in and out of the processing mode, I did the bulk of my work with a busy, overactive mind.

My typical therapy session went something like this. My client would say something and I would deliberately search through my memories for the "right" response. The client would say something else and again I'd be back in my memory, actively searching for the "appropriate" response. This would continue for the majority of the session. Granted, I had learned the model so well that most of my deliberate memory searches were imperceptible to my clients. In other words, if you were watching us you would have seen what would have appeared to be a natural flow of exchanges. In reality, however, I wasn't doing therapy guided by the stream. I was actively intervening, and deliberately using my mind like a computer, to mechanically process my memories. Thus, my experience of doing therapy was usually stressful...often draining.

Overusing the processing mode is typical for most therapists. That's why the burnout rate for our profession is so high. When my level of understanding was low, I used to think that the stress came from the therapy. Now, I realize that the stress, or lack of it, is determined by the particular mode of thinking that's guiding the therapist.

It's helpful to recognize that the particular thoughts that a person is habitually processing doesn't really matter. Even the most pleasant, uplifting, or useful thought in the world, processed chronically, will produce the feeling of boredom.   Deliberately holding onto any memories for too long takes people into lower quality mental functioning.   Consider the teenage girl, for example, who won't stop thinking about a boy she recently met at school. Day and night she dwells on him and "how wonderful he is."   She can't seem to get him out of her mind.   He's in her thoughts every minute of the day.   Engulfed in these "wonderful" memories, she forgets her homework, ignores her friends, and stops eating.   What some might call "puppy love," is actually a case of the mental flu caused by overused processing thinking.

In the same way that smoking interferes with the natural ability of our lungs to breathe in their innate, healthy way, or that bad cholesterol can block our heart from pumping in its natural, healthy manner, or that leaving the emergency brake on can wear down the engine of a car, overused processing thinking puts an incredible strain on our mental functioning.   To the degree that we allow the processing mode to become the master or director of our thinking, our psychological functioning suffers.   It becomes mechanized, redundant, stressed, or even dysfunctional in the same way that our body can lose its tone, become fatigued, worn out, even seriously diseased when unhealthy physical habits interfere with the natural, healthy operation of our heart, lungs, and other vital organs.

Unfortunately, most of us have innocently learned to vastly overuse Mode Two.   In fact, in this culture, what we typically refer to as thinking is processing thinking.   Why?   For one thing, most people (including most psychologists) aren't even aware of free-flowing thinking because it is effortless and invisible.   Processing thinking, on the other hand, is obvious, because it takes conscious effort.   Thus, the processing mode is what most people in this culture have come to see not only as "normal" thinking, but the only mode of thinking available to them.   For most of us, Mode Two has become the master or director of our thinking.

Processing Mode Abuse #2 - Misuse

Processing thinking is also abused when people learn to misuse it by indiscriminately processing misleading, dysfunctional, or "painful" information. As you journeyed through life, it's likely that you used processing thinking to learn and store in your memory some less functional, fallacious, even superstitious and "painful" thought programs. The following list illustrates the themes of some of the many varieties of dysfunctional thought programs that people innocently learn. When these useless thought chains are brought to life through the misuse of processing thinking, they can cause us great distress, interfere with our objectivity, sour our personal relationships, and shatter our contentment. Are any of these conditioned thought programs stored in the files of your memory?

You can't trust men.

Women are only interested in marriage.

I need an intimate relationship to be happy.

I'm always suspicious when things get too good.

If you don't worry, something awful will happen.

I'll finally be happy when I have children.

Men never show their sensitive side.

A good mother always sacrifices for her family.

If my husband really loved me he'd know what I want.

I could never forgive a person who cheated on me.

Winter is depressing.

Wasting time is unforgivable.

People should always do their best.

It's important to be liked by everyone.

Living life is stressful.

I have to get my needs met in order to be happy.

Without my job I'd be nothing.

Lazy people make me angry.

People should pride themselves on their appearance.

Failing at something is awful.

Negative feelings build character.

Winning is the most important thing.

The past limits our future.

It's helpful to recognize that these dysfunctional thought programs can only cause us distress when we misuse Mode Two and start deliberately processing them. In the processing mode, a person's mind is filled with thoughts from his memory. Thus, while he's in Mode Two, his feelings are always the shadow of the memories he's processing. If these memories are painful... the more he processes them, the more pain he experiences. The more painful his memories, the more agonizing his pain. It's that simple.

Think about a time in your life when your thinking became loud and deliberate. A time when you were obsessed with or fixated on some event or activity. It might have been a sport or a game that you were playing. Perhaps it was a work assignment. It could have been an argument with your spouse or sweetheart. Whatever it was, it was a time when your thinking became loud and deliberate, a time when your mind shifted into a state of alert and was ready to pounce.

It may have felt like you had tunnel vision. Everywhere you looked you saw only your thoughts in action about this particular issue or event. These thoughts had you tightly in their grip...you just couldn't seem to shake them or let them go. Perhaps you were working diligently to analyze a situation. You may have been trying desperately to figure out what to do, agonizing to prove your point, struggling to find a solution, laboring urgently to come up with the "right" answer. Yet, nothing seemed to click. The more you strained to figure things out, or to find evidence for your view, the more frustrated, lost, and confused you became. Minutes may have seemed like hours. You felt a tremendous load of tension and distress. At the end of your activity, even if you found some answers, you felt exhausted and drained!

We've all misused the processing mode and kept painful thoughts alive. Here's a winning entry from me. I was with a group of friends on a golf trip in northern Michigan. On the morning of our first golf day I went to the driving range to practice. I started off hitting a few shots with my pitching wedge and everything was fine. Then I grabbed my seven iron and made what I thought was a good swing. I couldn't believe what happened. Quickly, I put another ball in place, and took a nice, easy pass. A hot, flashing wave of mild terror radiated up my entire body. It was the "golfer's nightmare." I had "shanked" two shots in a row!

For you non-golfers, a "shank" is when you hit the golf ball with an iron club and, if you're a left-handed golfer like me, the ball flies off the club head almost ninety degrees to the left. I tried my best to put my fearful memories out of my mind. I tried to convince myself that it was just a fluke. I mean there's a big difference between shanking two shots in a row and "having the dreaded shanks!"

I took a few deep breaths, stretched a bit, closed up the face on my seven iron, and set up another ball. Slowly and easily, I took back the club and unloaded...another SHANK. Quickly, I set up another ball...SHANK. Another ball...SHANK. Three more balls...SHANK, SHANK, SHANK!

My thoughts ran wild. I couldn't believe it. How could this have happened? I don't shank. I never shank. What the heck was I doing? I started analyzing, trying desperately to figure it out. I felt a sense of urgency...our tee time was only ten minutes away. What was I going to do? I changed my stance, I tried other clubs, I adjusted my swing plane, I altered my distance from the ball, I loosened my grip, I tried a different back swing, I slowed down my swing speed...SHANK, SHANK, SHANK!!

Finally, I made my way to the first tee, feeling hopeless and discouraged. My mind was spinning with angry, negative, conflicting thoughts. It was the worst round of golf I'd ever played. I hardly noticed the trees, the sky, or the clouds. I didn't feel the warm breezes, smell the lilac bushes, or joke with my friends. I felt horribly self-conscious and was very negative the entire day. The round seemed like it took eight hours to finish. At the end of play I was depressed, exhausted, and drained!

Most people don't realize that the presence of psychological pain always means that they're misusing the processing mode and misguidedly short-circuiting the natural, free-flowing source of their innate mental health. Not understanding what they're doing, most people come to accept or tolerate the lower quality life experiences they are inadvertently causing themselves by habitually misusing their processing thinking. Judy Sedgeman cites a typical example of the heavy price many people pay for this innocent lack of understanding:

> "...A tennis player who moves through her game seemingly intuitively might leave the court and become frantic in the face of an angry loved one. As she engaged in more and more thinking about how difficult the situation was, she would lose the confidence and ease she had displayed on the court only moments before. Frightened by her insecure feelings, she would try to think her way out of the situation, relying on experience and knowledge, engaging in habitual 'processing mode' thinking which consistently produces the same behavior, thus keeping her in a spiral of ever-escalating 'processing mode' thinking. It would not be obvious to her that she is using two completely different thought modes in each situation, and that the mode of thinking that produces her experience of tennis would produce an equally exhilarating experience of any aspect of life if she understood it and learned to access it."

To the degree that people innocently misuse the processing mode to habitually process less functional, often "painful" thoughts, they tend to become gripped by the lower quality List B feelings and perceptions that they are unknowingly bringing to life. In other words, if our thought recognition is low, and we misuse the processing mode, we're much more likely to react to the skewed perceptions and insecure feelings that we're temporarily experiencing. For example, if a person's spouse is late for dinner, and he's misusing Mode Two, it's likely that he'll become gripped by his biased memories in action. Depending on the particular thoughts that he's squeezing, it could appear to him that she's a jerk...or that she's having an affair...or that she's deliberately trying to upset him...or that she doesn't love him anymore. The less thought recognition he has, the more likely it is that he'll continue misusing the processing mode, and become even more distressed.

If you get fired from your job and start processing some frightening thoughts, it's going to be painful. Depending on the thoughts you're squeezing, it could look like you're a failure...or that life's unfair...or that your luck is always bad...or even that your boss deserves to be shot! If your level of understanding is low, you might even begin designing your life around the distorted List B perspectives activated by misusing Mode Two thinking.

Also, if you misuse the processing mode, life can start to look very personal. For example, if the man you ask out on a date says, "No," it's likely to seem personal. Depending on the thoughts that you're processing, it might appear that you're unattractive...or that you're a loser...or that you're going to be a lonely spinster. When you're misusing the processing mode, and don't realize what you're doing, you're likely to become gripped by the momentary illusion of how personal things look.

Finally, when people misuse Mode Two, they're often at the effect of their thoughts about what hasn't yet happened, what should have happened, or what's likely to happen. These thoughts in action create the illusions of needs, wants, urges, and problems which, with little thought recognition, can appear to require immediate satisfaction or urgent attention.

On the other hand, there can never be chronic stress or distress in free-flowing thinking. Why? Because in Mode One, thoughts glide through the mind rather than stagnate in the mind. Also, since Mode One is always responsive to the moment, any memory (even a painful one) that comes to mind in this mode will come and go usefully. George Pransky puts it this way:

"...Because these thoughts (painful ones) are flowing, they do not provide the potential for chronic stress and distress. We might have a memory of a childhood trauma or a thought of conscience that we mistreated someone without realizing it. We might feel sadness for the loss of a loved one. All these thoughts are painful, but they would not cause chronic pain because they will flow through the person's mind and actually be evolved and healed in the process. We might see a person in distress and have a bittersweet feeling of compassion. There might be a painful thought in the moment, but the free-flowing mode thinking protects us from chronic stress. Chronic stress and distress can only happen in the context of the processing mode within the thoughts that are deliberately held in mind and processed for a period of time."

Thus, if your spouse is late for dinner and your thinking is free-flowing, you'll always view the situation with more wisdom, compassion, and common sense. For example, it's likely that you'll realize that her behavior wasn't intentional. Perhaps you'll appreciate how hard she works and the heavy traffic she encounters each evening. If you get the thought that she's having an affair, it will be followed by another thought that will put things in perspective. If you get fired from your job and you're thinking in Mode One, you'll likely see it in a more hopeful way, perhaps as an opportunity to explore new, even bigger possibilities.

Also, when you're in free-flowing thinking, things won't look personal. Whatever happens in your life, it's not going to look personal. If you ask a woman out on a date and she says no, in the free-flowing mode it won't seem personal. You won't be tempted to analyze or question her response. You'll likely realize that not every woman's thoughts will create you as desirable. Thus, you'll simply look for another woman to ask out or find something else to do.

Finally, when you're thinking in Mode One, you'll feel complete and fulfilled no matter what the circumstances in your life. You won't hold onto or entertain thoughts that enter your mind about what's missing or not right in your life. Thus, the illusions of wants, needs, urges, and problems won't take form.

The Puzzle of the Nine Dots

Another helpful way to illustrate the limitations of misused Mode Two thinking is the "puzzle of the nine dots." In this puzzle, there are nine dots in the configuration below. To solve the puzzle, you have to connect all nine dots using only four straight lines. If you haven't seen this puzzle before, please give it a try.

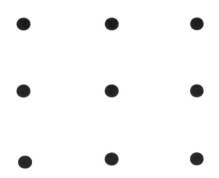

It's not as easy as you might think to connect all nine dots with just four straight lines. For most people, one of the dots always seems to escape connection. Why is it so difficult for most people to see a solution to this puzzle? For one thing, most people tend to deliberately look for solutions in Mode Two. They start actively processing the puzzle through the thoughts in their memory. By so doing, people tend to get visually trapped within the square or "box shape" that's formed by connecting the puzzle's eight outer dots. This limited view, kept alive via processing thinking, keeps most people looking for solutions within the confines of the box shape of the outer dots. Thus, most people keep trying solution after solution by connecting the dots using lines like they would use in a game of "tic-tac-toe."

Below, I've presented one of the many possible solutions to the puzzle of the nine dots. Realizing this solution, however, requires a shift in perspective...one generated from the stream of fresh thought that precedes one's memories. Seeing this solution requires that people stop deliberately processing, clear their mind, and move back to the stream. By accessing their responsive, free-flowing thinking, people are empowered to notice solutions that their memories won't let them see.

A similar shift in thinking mode is necessary for people to break free from other limiting reality illusions inadvertently created and maintained by misusing Mode Two. Take the illusion of a fixed personality trait, for example. I've illustrated this within the puzzle solution below. Please imagine that the "box" formed by connecting the eight outer dots of the puzzle contains all of the possible realities that a person can create by processing their memories. Put another way, in Mode Two, a person can only see his memories in action. Let's say that a person who thinks chronically in Mode Two has the thought in his memory that he is "very shy." Now imagine a time in that same person's life when a "bold" and "very assertive" response would make perfect sense. As you can see below, the thoughts for these more sensible responses lie outside of his box of memories. In other words, this person has no stored memories for being "bold" or "assertive."

The key to seeing creative solutions to the puzzle of the nine dots is the same key that's necessary to see beyond the limits of other reality illusions spawned by habitually processing our memories. The key is a shift in understanding, one that allows us to stop misusing processing thinking. One that allows us to access the fresh, responsive, free-flowing stream of thought that precedes our memory. Using our two modes of thinking in the way they were meant to be used will provide us all with the fresh, original thoughts and useful memories we need to answer life's requests and solve life's puzzles in more effective, creative, compassionate, common sense ways!

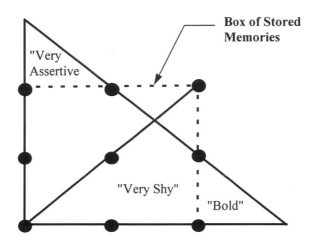

Thinking Like a Kid Again

I can remember a time when I offered to show some of my therapy clients a quick way to find several common sense solutions to their "problems," and save themselves a lot of time and worry in the process. Most became curious and asked me to explain. What I told them was this. First, they had to go to my waiting room or down the street to the nearby elementary school and borrow a healthy five- or six-year-old child. Second, they had to describe their problem to the child, stating "just the facts." Then they would simply ask the child exactly what they should do to resolve the problem.

Two clients actually took me up on this suggestion. One was a 40-year-old man named Don who came to therapy feeling quite depressed and anxious after being fired from an influential, high-paying job. Don made a mistake in judging the income potential of a business that his company had purchased on his recommendation. The business went "belly up," and his boss fired him. He was so depressed and angry that it was difficult for Don to even start looking for a new job. During our second session, it occurred to me to make him "the offer."

Don lightened up at my suggestion, smiled, and to my surprise said, "Okay, let's try it." My next client that day just happened to have brought her five-year-old son, Jeremy, with her. Jeremy was a very bright, outgoing, happy child. He knew me from some of her past visits and was willing, even eager, when I asked him to help.

I brought Jeremy into my office and introduced him to Don. Just the presence of this happy child, full of life and enthusiasm, seemed to raise Don's mood even more. I told Jeremy that Don needed some help with a problem and would like some advice. Jeremy was ready to play and inquisitively asked Don, "What's your problem?"

Don did quite well sticking to the facts. He started out saying something like, "Well Jeremy, I had this job that I really liked and I made a lot of money. Then I made a big mistake and my boss fired me. Now I'm really sad and angry. I'm not sure what to do." The conversation between Jeremy and Don continued like this:

Jeremy: "Did you tell your boss that you were sorry and ask him to take you back?"

Don: "Yes, I did, but he wouldn't let me stay."

Jeremy: "I think you should find a nicer boss to work for."

Don: "Actually, he was a really good boss, I just made a really big, dumb mistake."

Jeremy: "Well, that's okay. Everybody makes mistakes. My mom says mistakes are good so we can learn new things."

Don: "I know, but I should have known better. I was really stupid."

Jeremy: "It's okay to do dumb things. I do them all the time. You need to just forget about it and find another job."

Don: "You're probably right...but it's just not that easy."

Jeremy: "It shouldn't be that hard...you really seem nice and smart to me. How many jobs have you asked for?"

Don: "Well, none yet."

Jeremy: "Then how do you know it's hard?"

I think you get the idea. Jeremy was a pretty bright, healthy child. He thought primarily in the free-flowing mode. Thus, he often displayed a wisdom beyond his years. At one time or another, almost everyone has been blown away by the striking clarity and common sense in a healthy child's view of life. With their free-flowing thinking typically at the helm, the perspective of healthy children isn't limited by their memories. Thus, they are typically masters at seeing life's more obvious and sensible possibilities.

Compared to Don, Jeremy hadn't learned to chronically squeeze his memories, painful or otherwise. Thus, Jeremy's view wasn't distorted by a maze of processing mode activated, biased thoughts about "getting fired," "making mistakes," or "looking for new jobs." With his thinking free-flowing, several simple, common sense solutions for Don's "problem" were obvious to Jeremy. No big deal!

Don, however, like most of the people I see in therapy, had a pretty low level of thought recognition. Thus, he was innocently stuck in the grip of the painful reality illusions that he was innocently creating by misusing the processing mode. Living in the frightening feelings spawned by those painful memories in action, Don was trying desperately to find a way out. With limited understanding, however, it was difficult for Don to slow down, clear his mind, and allow his natural, intelligent, free-flowing thinking to show him a way.

Principles Don't Care What People Think

To sum things up, here's a blunt, yet helpful analogy. Let's say that you go to your local hardware store, buy an electrical wiring kit and bring it home. If you clearly understand and follow the instructions to the letter, place the wires according to the natural design principles of electricity, the lights will go on, the buzzers will buzz, and everything will work perfectly. On the other hand, if you misunderstand the instructions and mistakenly get your wires crossed, you'll get no lights and no buzzing buzzers. What's worse, you might get shocked or even electrocuted!

Successfully plugging in to the natural experience of healthy psychological functioning works in much the same way. If you understand and follow your human psychological design principles and allow your mind to guide you in its natural, free-flowing way, you'll automatically get List A psychological functioning. On the other hand, if you innocently start abusing your processing thinking and short-circuit Mode One, you'll instantly get psychological breakdown and perhaps a whole lot of List B pain and suffering!

The principles of human psychological functioning don't care what you think about them anymore than the principles of electricity care about what you think. Principles are principles...facts are facts. If you clearly understand them, respect and follow them, things always work much better. If you don't clearly recognize and follow them, innocent or not, things will malfunction. If you jump out the second floor window of a building, gravity doesn't care what you think, it just pulls you down...splat! If you mistakenly learn to abuse Mode Two thinking, the principles of psychological functioning don't care that you didn't know...they'll just spiral you downward...bam! How good can you stand it!

Chapter 10

Common Misuses of the "Processing Mode"

N ow you understand how overusing and misusing the processing mode acts as a mental health contaminator. The processing of our memories was designed to occur under the intelligent direction of the free-flowing mode. As long as we allow Mode One to guide us in and out of Mode Two, our present moments will always be rich and full.

Ann, a former client of mine, envisioned the wise, effortless guidance of her natural, flowing thinking in the following unique way. She imagined herself basking in the warm sun on a magnificent raft, floating on a quiet stream of peaceful, gliding thought. Standing at the end of the raft, baton in hand, was Leonard Bernstein, the famous symphony orchestra conductor. Ann, in a state of complete relaxation, fully trusted Leonard to masterfully direct the free-flowing symphony of her thinking. With a flick of his baton, he would summon up fresh, original thought melodies from the stream. When appropriate, he would direct the processing of thought notes from her memory, always in just the right key.

When her processing drums began beating too loudly, Ann would notice the intelligent thought, "Leave it to Leonard." Immediately, she would clear her mind, and trust the guidance of the free-flowing stream.

Whenever we deliberately leave the stream and start indiscriminately processing our memories, our experience of life always becomes more stressful. Unfortunately, most people in this culture don't have the level of understanding needed to trust their free-flowing thinking to guide them in and out of the processing mode. Most of us have learned to chronically overuse and misuse Mode Two. What's even more unfortunate, most of us don't even realize what we're doing. When people's level of understanding is low, they can't see that the source of all their psychological stress and unhappiness is the abuse of processing thinking. On the other hand, there can never be chronic stress and distress in Mode One. In the words of George Pransky:

> "Mode One - free-flowing thinking does not necessarily produce positive, pleasurable thoughts. What characterizes this mode is not the content of the thoughts that pass through it, but rather the fact that these thoughts pass through, instead of being held and processed, as is the case in Mode Two. For example, a person might have a painful thought of anger in Mode One. Because it occurs in the free-flowing mode, however, that thought will pass through uneventfully, providing whatever knowledge or insight it imparts without the consequences of chronic distress. The same angry thought processed in Mode Two - processing thinking would result in chronic distress."

It's very helpful to recognize some of the more common, albeit treacherous, misuses of processing thinking that human beings innocently learn. Each of these lower quality thinking habits, when unrecognized and perpetuated, overrides our natural free-flowing thinking for no useful purpose. It's possible that you've learned some or even all of the lower grade Mode Two thinking habits that we'll visit in this chapter. By recognizing them for what they really are, you'll automatically start "leaving it to Leonard," and allowing the stream to guide you on a regular basis.

Processing Thoughts that Tie Your Worth to Externals

One insidious processing thinking habit involves deliberately processing thoughts that connect your personal worth to a variety of external events and circumstances. To get this lower quality thinking habit going, you first had to learn some superstitious thought programs that tie your self-worth to thoughts about your accomplishments, appearance, wealth, feelings, intelligence, toughness, opinions...just about anything external. You had to first learn the misleading idea that the source of your self-worth is located somewhere outside of you.

When processing mode-activated, this biased thought program produces, among other things, the uncomfortable experience of self-consciousness. First you learned your particular group of external worthiness thoughts from the long cultural list. Then, periodically you misused Mode Two to deliberately process these thoughts and analyze your self-worth. When people don't realize what they're doing, this low quality thinking habit can trap them in obsessive rituals of self-absorbed assessment, self-monitoring, and self-analysis. Perform, assess, rate...perform, assess, judge...observe, judge, and figure your worth. Doesn't sound very peaceful or serene, does it?

I can certainly relate to this insidious misuse of processing thinking. Very early on, I innocently began foolishly short-circuiting my easy, free-flowing thinking by getting really good at this one. I guess it began when I was about two years old. My mother and grandfather used to spend hours reading to me from a Mother Goose book of poems and nursery rhymes. This book had pictures and drawings to illustrate the themes of wonderful poems like "How Would You Like To Go Up In A Swing?," "I Eat My Peas With Honey," "The Owl and the Pussycat," "Wynken, Blynken, and Nod," and my favorite, "The Night Before Christmas." Members of my family read these poems to me over and over again, perhaps hundreds of times.

One day, when I was about two and a half, an interesting thing happened. I took the book to my grandfather, asking him if I could read the poems. Grandpa agreed, and as my mother tells it, "He nearly fainted!" Why? Because I recited just about every poem in the book, almost word for word, turning each page at nearly the right time!

What happened here? I couldn't read, so I wasn't actually reading. What occurred was that I had intuitively learned most of the poems. I hadn't done it purposely and I wasn't trying to prove anything. It was simply the outcome of my natural interest, enjoyment, fascination, and total immersion in the experience of being read to by my family. Since my mind was operating primarily in the free-flowing mode, I was naturally enjoying life and happened to effortlessly memorize the poems.

At that point in my life, I hadn't yet learned any thoughts that this accomplishment meant something personal about me. Thoughts connecting my self-worth to my poem-reciting ability, or any other ability for that matter, hadn't yet been added to my memory. My natural, free-flowing thinking was solidly at the helm, doing its job to effortlessly create a full, joyous experience of life. Heck, I didn't even know that I was enjoying life. I was simply immersed in the natural, high quality experience of living that's automatically produced by Mode One - free-flowing thinking.

For my parents, however, this event took on a somewhat different meaning. You see, they were wonderful "normal parents." This means that they had already learned the habit of deliberately processing thoughts that tied their parental self-worth to externals. In this culture, the main entree on the "parent prove yourself processing menu" is thoughts about their children. To some degree, most parents in this culture have learned to deliberately process thoughts that connect their worth to their children's attributes like appearance, intelligence, athletic ability, and manners.

You can probably see that my poem-reciting ability was a "blue plate special item" on the "parent prove your worth thought processing menu." Imagine, a two-and-a-half-year-old son who knows over a hundred poems by heart. Some really long ones too. Some with big words, no less. He recites them on request with tremendous feeling and enthusiasm. A parent's "prove your worth processing feast" if there ever was one!

Here's what happened. At the time, my father worked at WXYZ radio station in Detroit. He helped produce some of the old classic radio programs like "The Lone Ranger" and "The Green Hornet." He saw a perfect way to do it. He taped a segment with me reciting some of the poems and presented it to his station manager. The manager liked the concept and a few weeks later, on a Sunday afternoon, the first broadcast of "The Little Tommy Kelley Show" aired coast-to-coast on the Mutual Broadcasting Network!

I don't remember any of this, but my mother tells me that the weekly half-hour program ran for about six months. During that time, I received boxes of letters and postcards from fans of the show. The broadcast was written up in several local and national magazines and newspapers. I was often characterized as a child prodigy. In other words, I started getting loads of attention from my parents, other people, and the media tied to my performance on the show.

Here's the point in sharing this experience with you. Initially, my poem reciting was an example of the joyous and creative things that children do spontaneously when their healthy free-flowing thinking is in full gear, and they're totally absorbed in the experience of living. My initial motivation for memorizing the poems and recording the radio show with my father was the joy, curiosity, and enthusiasm naturally created by living life in the stream.

However, as I began to notice the reactions of my parents and others to my performance, I started learning thoughts that it meant something personal about me. I started storing away memories that I must be "special" or "unique." I noticed the responses of all these people to my performing and I started collecting thoughts that I must be an important or special person because of my ability to perform.

Over time, this initial thought trickle grew into a cascade of thoughts that connected my self-worth to my performance. When I would leave the stream and start deliberately processing these thoughts, they would generate a variety of List B highs and lows. By the time I started school, I had gotten pretty good at this processing mode misuse. For example, I would frequently process thoughts that I had to get all A's to be worthwhile. Thus, I felt lots of anxiety during my early school years. If I thought a teacher was upset with me, I literally couldn't sleep at night. I coped with these insecure emotions by over-preparing for exams. I would read each chapter four or five times. If I had to, I would even cheat to stay on top.

On weekends, following a successful exam grade, my habitual processing might slow down temporarily. For a short while, I'd feel more relaxed and peaceful. It wouldn't be long, however, (usually early Sunday evening) before it would kick back in once again. Instantly, I'd start feeling anxious, and off I'd go, studying compulsively. As time went by, I shifted from spending most of my moments enjoying life (thinking predominantly in the free-flowing mode), to wasting most of my moments trying to "prove my worth" (misusing the processing mode and being gripped by the biased perceptions and insecure emotions it spawned)!

Processing "Painful" Thoughts Connected To Common Life Experiences

Another common processing thinking misuse involves learning and deliberately processing biased, often painful thoughts connected to common life experiences such as intimacy, risk-taking, change, being alone, authority, succeeding, or failing. When processing mode activated, these biased thoughts can produce an array of insecure emotions, like guilt, anxiety, depression, and anger.

One poignant example of this Mode Two thinking misuse involved a child named Nicholas, who was observed in Chicago at the Erickson Institute for Advanced Study in Child Development. Nicholas had a horrible habit of approaching other kids in his nursery school class as if he were going to kiss them. Instead of kissing them, however, he would bite them!

The researchers went back and reviewed videos of Nicholas at twenty months interacting with his mother, who had been diagnosed schizophrenic. They found that she had responded to Nicholas' every expression of anger with compulsive kisses. The researchers dubbed them "kisses of death," and their true significance was obvious to Nicholas, who in these videos arched his back in horror at her approaching lips. Years later, he passed his own learned rage onto his classmates.

Another good example involved a young man named Frank, one of my former therapy clients. Frank complained that he was a "neat freak." He said that unless everything in his car, home, and office was orderly and in place, he would feel anxious and insecure. Also, he demanded the same orderly behavior from his girlfriend, who finally got so fed up with his constant complaints that she threatened to leave him if he didn't get some help. Frank had tried for years to be less compulsive about neatness. Some days were better than others, but this frustrating habit seemed to follow him around like his own shadow.

During the course of counseling, Frank recalled an incident from his past that he thought might be related to his present predicament. He was about five years old, playing in the family room with his older brothers, ages seven and nine. Sometime earlier, his mother had told the boys to stop playing and clean up the room. When his mother returned and found them still horsing around, she apparently over-reacted and said something like, "If you guys don't get this room spotless right now, I'm going to leave and you won't have a mother anymore." To Frank's recollection, the brothers immediately straightened the room.

Later, however, an interesting thing happened.   Around midnight, the nine-year-old brother got up to use the bathroom and found little Frank sitting in the bathtub attempting to clean it! His older brother ran to the mother's bedroom, awakened her, and led her to the bathroom. The mother, obviously in a better mood, picked up Frank from the tub, told him that he didn't have to clean it, and lovingly tucked him into bed.

It occurred to Frank, that as a child he must have learned some thoughts that connected his well-being and security to making sure that things were neat and clean. He remembered that his mother also had "a thing about neatness." He recalled that her favorite saying was, "Cleanliness is next to Godliness." Frank saw that when he misused Mode Two to process these biased thoughts, he experienced painful emotions like guilt and anxiety. He realized that he was spending much of his time misusing the processing mode, deliberately analyzing, worrying, and surveying his surroundings to make sure everything was in the right place!

Another client, Ryan, came to see me with the complaint that it was very difficult for him to work in groups. For example, Ryan said he was fine at work until his boss assigned him to participate in group projects. These group assignments caused him incredible amounts of anxiety.

Recently, one of his college instructors had his class break up into small groups to do term projects. Ryan tried his best to convince the instructor to let him work alone on a term paper. The professor insisted, however, that working in groups was one of the main objectives of the class. Ryan thought about withdrawing from the course but needed it to graduate. Instead, he entered therapy to find out once and for all why he was "such a loner," and felt so anxious in certain groups of people.

During our conversations together, Ryan also remembered an incident from his past that seemed to be related to his present predicament. He recalled being about nine years old, walking down the street with his father. His dad suggested that they have a race to the corner, about a block away. They started running, and just before reaching the corner, his father purposely tripped him. Ryan fell to the ground, badly skinning both knees. His father completed the race and won!

Not a very nice thing for a father to do to a son, but such things happen. Anyway, it occurred to Ryan that he must have learned some biased thoughts about trusting other people. Later, he recalled that his father was also pretty much a loner. He remembered that both of his parents were very cautious about trusting other people. It finally dawned on Ryan that his tendency to avoid groups was his way of coping with the insecure emotions produced by misusing Mode Two to process these biased memories.

Processing Painful Memories Related to "Traumas"

Most people who experience horrible events like rape, child abuse, natural disasters, or seeing a co-worker or loved one assaulted or murdered, come away with some extremely painful memories. For many of these people, something that reminds them of the original event will often trigger these awful recollections. If kept alive through misused Mode Two thinking, these memories will sustain the horrible feelings and perceptions connected with the original event.

Sometimes, the initial incident experienced as "traumatic" may not seem to be all that significant. Consider my client, Liz, for example, who told me the following story. Liz, a 27-year-old college student at a local university, was sitting at her desk on the first day of her American History class. Being a "history buff," Liz was in a very good mood, looking forward to starting the course.

Her history professor arrived a few minutes late. He was a tall, thin man, about 60 years old, with a white beard. Upon looking up and making eye contact with the professor, Liz started feeling incredibly anxious. Her heart began pounding and her hands got sweaty. She became so uncomfortable and self-conscious that she finally had to get up and leave the room!

Liz tried her best to calm down in a nearby lounge. A few minutes later she attempted to go back in to her classroom. However, when she glanced at the professor through the window of the classroom door, her panicky feelings resumed. Feeling very "shook up" and "confused" about this incident, Liz decided to consult with me to find out what had happened.

After reassuring Liz that there was nothing wrong with her mental health, I explained to her about thought and the two modes of thinking. I suggested to Liz that she may have had some painful memories re-activated by this event. While stressing that it wasn't important to look for the original source of these memories, she might want to notice if any similar event from her past happened to occur to her between sessions. I requested that she not dwell on it or try to figure it out, just to be open to any recollection that might show up for her.

At our next session, Liz shared the following story. Her mother had recalled the following event from Liz's childhood. When Liz was about four years old, she was riding her tricycle on the sidewalk near her home. Apparently she hit a bump and lost her balance. Falling off her trike, she hit her head pretty hard on the sidewalk. A man walking on the other side of the street ran across to see if she was okay. Her mother, about a half block away, also saw Liz fall and came running at about the same time. Little Liz, hurt, frightened, and slightly dazed from the fall, looked up at the stranger bending over her and panicked. Urgently, she struggled to her feet and ran sobbing and shaking into her mother's arms. Her mother remembered the Samaritan because he was very tall and thin and had this long white beard!

Modeling the "Processing Mode" Thinking Misuses of Others

Many other habitual processing mode thinking misuses are learned from watching and modeling other people like our parents or parental figures. For example, if one or both of your parents habitually misused Mode Two to process thoughts that created feelings of frustration or anger, you may have learned this "bad temper" thinking habit as well. If one of your parents was always analyzing people, figuring things out, or compulsively planning their life, you may have picked up this obsessive, "busy mind" processing habit yourself. If your parents worried chronically or habitually judged and found fault with just about everything, you may have learned these processing thinking misuses as well. Allan Flood talks about acquiring his mother's habit of worrying:

> "...My mother is the quintessential worrier. When I told her yesterday I was finding time to study for an exam while I was walking the dog, her immediate response was to warn me to be careful and not trip and hurt myself. So when growing up, I learned the tendency to "squeeze" thoughts of potential danger by worrying about them - holding them in my mind longer than necessary. Thought recognition gives me the perspective to disrespect these thoughts and not squeeze them as hard - to have faith in my deeper intelligence to look for the rocks."

Even very young children learn by imitation, by watching how others act, especially when they see someone in distress. Think about it. As a child, did you learn any low quality processing mode thinking habits from the significant people in your life? Each of these habitual misuses of the processing mode uselessly overrides our natural design to think primarily in a responsive, free-flowing way.

Imagine, a whole slew of processing mode activated, insecure emotion/reactive behavior vicious circles spinning around and around, over and over and over again, hundreds, perhaps thousands of times during the course of a person's lifetime. Since each of these vicious circles requires the misuse of processing thinking to keep them revolving, people innocently spend more and more time misusing the processing mode. By so doing, they end up habitually short-circuiting the natural, healthy operation of their gift of thought!

The "Circle of Wise and Sensible Possibilities"

Please let me slice it up one more way. You started out thinking typically at the speed of life. You started out experiencing life primarily through the pristine perspective of high quality, healthy, free-flowing thinking. Thus, your typical view of life was a vast array of wise, sensible, and joyous possibilities. Immersed in a rich, free-flowing supply of fresh, original thoughts and responsive memories, you started out with a typically high quality perspective from which to view your options in life. Most of the time, you saw life's landscape with clarity, common sense, and wisdom. You felt free to go anywhere, and do anything that was sensible and productive. I've used the circle below to represent people's typical view of life when the free-flowing mode is the master or director of their thinking. I've called it the "Circle of Wise and Sensible Possibilities."

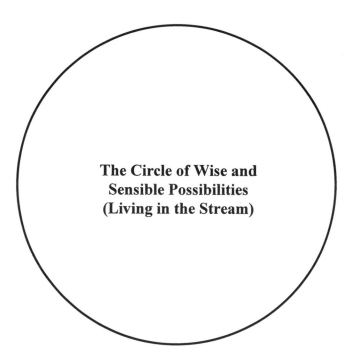

**The Circle of Wise and
Sensible Possibilities
(Living in the Stream)**

**Free-Flowing Mode the Master
Processing Mode the Servant**

As time passed, however, it's likely that you learned your particular ways of misusing processing thinking. For example, you may have learned to worry chronically, to think in a wandering, ambivalent way, to become a habitual "fault-finder," or to think perfectionistically. Possibly, you cultivated an analytical, "busy mind" processing habit, or learned to habitually calculate your worth based on your performance. Thus, over time, it's possible that you, like me, began spending less time experiencing life fully in each moment (thinking predominantly in the free-flowing mode) and more time feeling self-conscious and distressed (chronically misusing the processing mode)!

When people have a low level of understanding, their low quality, processing mode thinking habits take on a life of their own. Increasingly, they short-circuit or override their natural, intelligent, free-flowing thinking. Thus, in virtually no time flat, people's typical view of life's landscape as a smorgasbord of wise and sensible possibilities starts to narrow and wither. More and more, certain areas of the "Circle of Wise and Sensible Possibilities" begin to appear like "danger zones" to be avoided, perhaps at all cost.

Say, for example, that you (like me) learned the following superstitious thought program, " To be worthwhile, you always have to do your best." When I was growing up, my mother would frequently tell me, "You can only do your best...that's all you can do!" I know now, that she was just trying to be supportive and reassuring. Yet, when I would start indiscriminately processing my biased version of this thought, along with my other biased belief, "My worth depends on my performance," I ended up with a double whammy! When processing mode activated, these two biased thought programs would produce some really painful feelings. To cope, I got really good at doing only those things that I thought I did well. I would avoid other things at which I thought I might fail or even be average. Thus, certain areas in my "Circle of Wise and Sensible Possibilities" like "being average is okay," or "failing is okay," or "new things to try" became off-limits for me most of the time!

The "Box of Limited Possibility"

The less responsive, often painful thoughts held in place by misused processing thinking start acting like one of those invisible electric fences. You've probably heard of them...the ones they use to keep pets and livestock inside certain boundaries. If an animal strays too far, he hits the invisible fence and gets zapped. In no time at all, the animal learns to avoid the "fence" at all cost!

With little thought recognition, the exact same result occurs for human beings. The distorted perceptions and painful feelings spawned by misused processing thinking can severely restrict the behaviors that people can see as possibilities. Thus, the areas on life's landscape in which people think they can safely play becomes limited. Poof...whole chunks of wise and sensible possibilities gone! Eventually, if people don't catch on to what they're doing, their view of life will slowly transform from the wondrous "Circle of Wise and Sensible Possibilities," to the claustrophobic "Box of Limited Possibility."

Processing Mode the Master
Free-Flowing Thinking Chronically Short-Circuited

Misguided Coping with Painful Feelings

When people have little thought recognition, they can't see how they got trapped inside the "Box of Limited Possibility." They don't know how to get out of the stifling, lower quality List B life experience that they are unknowingly producing by habitually misusing the processing mode. Thus, what do you imagine such people spend much of their time doing? That's right...they do their very best to cope. They try the best they can to deal with the redundant, predictable, stressful, unhappy, troubling, even tormenting view of life that they typically see when they innocently and habitually misuse Mode Two. Often, people cope by misguidedly trying to manipulate or change things "out there." Roger Mills, co-founder of Psychology of Mind, puts it this way:

"This manipulation could include hitting your spouse or children, picking a fight with someone, cheating, stealing, or otherwise trying to gain more control of your situation any way you can, or it could include drinking and using drugs. It could include self-pity as an attempt to feel better or obtain sympathy. It could include violence or lashing out verbally at others. It could include escaping into an inner world through delusional states or hallucinations."

When people have little or no understanding that misusing processing thinking is the source of their emotional pain, they find the best ways they can to feel better. People find ways to numb out, minimize, or distract themselves from the insecure emotions and unsettling perceptions that they themselves are unknowingly perpetuating by habitually abusing the processing mode.

That's right, each of my former "mental flu" symptoms (e.g., working seven jobs, avoiding commitment, worrying chronically about my appearance, compulsively striving to be special)...each of the presenting problems of my therapy client examples (e.g., mistrusting men, compulsive neatness, avoidance of group projects, anxiety about a professor, faking a kiss to bite people)...each of the misguided actions that you've been putting up with and can't seem to stop repeating...all of these so-called "dysfunctional behaviors," were the best ways we could see at the time to minimize the suffering that we misguidedly caused ourselves by misusing Mode Two! Again in the words of Roger Mills:

> "Those coping habits that arise through unrecognized processing mode thinking abuses can wreak havoc in our lives. When some people feel insecure, they light a cigarette. Others pour a Scotch and water. Others shoot up heroin or smoke crack. Others overeat. Others beat their wives or flirt with other people's wives. Others may pick a fight. Others may retreat into sullen withdrawal. The common denominator across all these self-destructive habits is that each is what the person has learned to do, or feel is the best they can do, when they are caught in the grip of processing mode-generated insecurity."

All of these misguided forms of coping represent the best ways that people can see to minimize their psychological pain when they don't understand about thought, the two thinking modes, and how their on-going experience of life is created. All forms of what psychologists call coping, neurotic, even psychotic behavior are simply the best ways that people have found to deal with the insecure feelings and frightening perceptions that arise when they innocently abuse the processing mode.

From your new level of understanding, you can now recognize your Mode Two thinking misuses for what they are. Now you can catch yourself when you start to slip back into them. Now you can better see when it's inappropriate to use processing thinking, or appropriate to allow the free-flowing mode to show you the way. Richard Carlson and Joe Bailey see it this way:

> "When we become frightened, we tend to return to the familiar--our habits, traditions, and memories. We tend to flip into the analytical mode. We churn, process, reprocess, mull over, and relive an

experience, over and over. This tendency is common to all of us, but it has never been productive. This is not what the analytical mode was meant for. Matters of the heart are generally better left to our original thought process. If we can't figure something out with analytical thinking in a few moments--or at most a few minutes--it's a good sign that we are in the wrong gear. The best strategy is to put the concern on the back burner. As we begin to sense when it's appropriate to stop using analytical thinking, the processing mode will become the servant of the free-flowing mode."

How good can you stand it!

———■———

Chapter 11

The Truth About Moods

C ongratulations...we've come a long way together on our journey to breakthrough understanding. I want to acknowledge you for your willingness to be coached with patience, humility, and a quiet mind. It's likely that some of the principles and concepts you've sampled thus far have been very different from those you previously held about human psychological functioning. Thank you for your willingness to consider this unique perspective.

I'm confident that your openness and humility has paid off with some profound shifts in your level of understanding. I'm certain that you recognize at a much deeper level that thought is the sole determinant of your moment to moment experience of life. Now, you realize that everything you see, feel, and do in life is always your thoughts in action!

Also, you can now see that how you use you're thinking is your access switch to pain and pleasure. Thinking primarily in the free-flowing mode is the one and only source of rich, fulfilling, and satisfying List A moments of now. Thinking primarily in Mode

One is the natural, healthy way your mind was designed to think. In fact, a human being living primarily in the wondrous experiences effortlessly created by free-flowing thinking, is who you truly are.

You started out in life thinking mostly in the free-flowing mode, typically experiencing high quality, List A levels of mental health. As time went by, however, it's likely that you learned your share of lower quality processing mode thinking habits. The more you innocently misused Mode Two, deliberately "squeezing" your memories, the more time you spent outside of the stream.

Finally, you now realize that to cope with the insecure feelings and distorted perceptions spawned by your processing thinking abuses, you likely engaged in some misguided behaviors, like trying to change yourself, other people, and things out there. Whatever you did to feel better, no matter how foolish or dysfunctional, it was the best choice you could see from the level of understanding you had at the time.

Except for some final, very helpful distinctions, you've now tried on the major principles and most of the core concepts of Psychology of Mind. When you clearly understand the true nature of moods, emotions, and higher-order feelings, you will then have all the pieces to the puzzle of human psychological functioning. These last distinctions are extremely useful ones. I can't wait to share them with you. Let's get started.

Confusion About Mood Fluctuations

Have you ever noticed how different life can appear depending on your mood? I've often marveled at how a mood shift could dramatically alter the appearance of even the most important things in my life. For example, when I'm in one of my lower moods, doing therapy always seems stressful, it often looks like I could find a better relationship partner, my close friends can seem selfish and inconsiderate, and my house often shows up like a huge money pit. In my higher moods, on the other hand, I wouldn't trade in the people, activities, and things in my life for anything. In a higher mood, I feel privileged to have a great profession, a wonderful, loving partner, several loyal, caring friends, and a charming, older house.

Most people don't clearly understand what moods really are. This was certainly true for me. For years, I didn't recognize the true meaning of mood fluctuations. Often, I was puzzled by the dramatic shifts in perspective that accompanied them. I thought that mood swings probably had something to do with people's personalities, their self-image, their character, or perhaps even their physiology or genes.

I was clear that all human beings experienced mood changes. During the course of a typical day, most people's moods shift up and down many times. Sometimes the source of a change in mood appeared to be attached to some external event like a death or a promotion. At other times, it seemed like moods had a life of their own. It looked as if a person's self-esteem, the quality of their feelings, and the state of their psychological well-being could shift up or down for no apparent reason.

Not clearly understanding moods was a big obstacle in my work. Most of the people I saw in therapy were often stuck in, at the effect of, or trying to cope with the painful stuff of their lower moods. A client might show up one week like Dr. Jekyll and the next like Mr. Hyde. At the beginning of a session a client might act mature and composed, and then suddenly transform into a "basket case." With little understanding about moods, I was often unsettled and bewildered by these sudden shifts.

The relationship conflicts of the couples I saw always seemed to occur when one or both partners was in a lower mood. It was almost exclusively in such moods that my clients would be tempted to do foolish, self-defeating, even destructive things. When I looked closely, I realized that the same was true for me!

Even more puzzling were my clients who, while appearing to be in higher moods, would still behave in nonsensical ways. Take Bill, for example, a very successful salesman who began therapy feeling very depressed and anxious about not making a sale for over two months. At our third session, Bill strided briskly into my office feeling extremely elated. His depressive symptoms had disappeared completely. Gleefully, Bill told me that he had finally made a huge sale that set him up financially for several months to come. I suggested that he could now take the much-needed vacation he had talked about, as his health was poor and his wife and children were feeling very neglected. To my surprise, however, Bill stated vehemently, "Are you kidding? I'm not going to take a minute off. I have to work even harder now. I've got a good chance to be Salesman of the Year."

Moods are Simply Changes in Our Thinking Quality

It wasn't until I understood the principles of Psychology of Mind that I finally realized the truth about moods. Moods are simply fluctuations in the overall quality of our thinking. Moods are changes in thinking quality that come and go for people at every level of understanding. For example, a person with a very high level of understanding, who spends virtually all of his time in free-flowing thinking, still has moods. Likewise, a person with a very low level of thought recognition, who almost continually misuses processing thinking, also experiences mood shifts.

A mood is noticeable to a person because it's a departure from what he would call his "normal" feeling state. For example, I began the introduction to this book by saying, "I used to be 'normal.' Like most people in this culture, I'd gotten used to living with several chronic symptoms of the mental flu." At that time in my life, my level of understanding was pretty low. Thus, the overall quality of my thinking was also quite low. I misused the processing mode to analyze my worth and performance on a pretty regular basis. Not surprisingly, therefore, my "normal" feeling state was somewhere in the vicinity of mild to moderate stress and anxiety. At that time, however, I didn't experience these lower quality feelings as a mood. They were "normal" for me. I didn't like them, but I'd gotten used to living with them as a way of life.

During those stressful times, it was "normal" for me to react to life, to regularly experience problems, needs, and urges, and to feel like I had something to prove. I typically saw life as hard work and I was usually pretty serious and intense. I had no idea back then that these less satisfying experiences were spawned by my lower quality processing mode habits of thinking. I didn't realize that they were the emotional highs and lows, and the biased perceptions that I was creating by habitually entertaining biased thoughts that tied my worth to my achievements, performance, successes, and failures. With the lower level of understanding I had in those days, this was simply how life looked to me. It was what I experienced as "normal."

At that time in my life, a low mood was feeling unhappy or perhaps troubled. When I was in an unhappy mood, the quality of my thinking would drop even lower than normal. I would begin deliberately squeezing some pretty depressing thoughts that created some very gloomy, pessimistic feelings. Not understanding then that it was just a mood, just a temporary change in my thinking quality, I typically became frightened and gripped by these lower quality perspectives. Often, I would berate myself for experiencing them. I mean, I'm a psychologist right? Psychologists aren't supposed to be unhappy! I'd wonder if I'd ever feel "normal" again. I'd start feeling dissatisfied with life, even cheated. I'd have little or no fun. To cope with these painful feelings, I would usually start working even more compulsively.

On the other hand, there were also times back then when my habitual processing thinking would quiet down. During those moments, my natural free-flowing thinking would kick in and temporarily I'd experience one of my higher moods. Suddenly, I'd feel more light-hearted, spontaneous, and have a nice, easy feeling of well-being. Life would appear to be more satisfying and fulfilling, even full of interesting possibilities. I'd feel more relaxed, was easy to be with, and started behaving in more sensible, responsive ways. Since my level of understanding then was pretty low, however, my higher moods didn't last very long. In a relatively short time, my processing thinking habits would kick back in, and back I'd go again to my "normal" experience of feeling stressed.

I'll never forget Sally, a client of mine who'd been diagnosed paranoid schizophrenic. Sally's "normal" feeling state was troubled, even tormented. Obviously, the typical quality of her thinking was very low. Sally thought almost constantly in the processing mode. She continually ruminated and obsessed about thoughts that were horribly frightening. Sally typically experienced her life through memories like, "My husband is going to poison me," "I have insects in my head that are eating my brain," and "I have superhuman intelligence." These thoughts in action produced hideous feelings for Sally like terror, rage, and paranoia. Also, they brought to life extreme perceptual distortions like paranoid delusions and grandiose hallucinations. Gripped by these distorted thoughts kept alive by her basement quality thinking, Sally often behaved in violent and self-destructive ways. At that time, this tormented experience of life was "normal" for Sally.

The case of Sally nicely illustrates the helpful understanding that moods are relative. In other words, a low mood for person "A" might be a very high mood for person "B." For example, feeling unhappy used to be my lowest mood. For Sally, however, who lived chronically in frightening, tormenting delusions and hallucinations, feeling unhappy was an extremely high mood.

On the other hand, for a person who typically feels joyful and exhilarated, a low mood might be the feeling of a sense of ease or contentment. These pleasant feelings that for many people would be a very high mood, would be experienced as a lower mood by a high functioning person whose thinking is almost always free-flowing. For poor Sally, however, a low mood might mean that she could see no other option but to contemplate suicide!

It's helpful to understand that when a person's level of understanding or thought recognition shifts upward, his overall thinking quality leaps forward as well. Why? Because with a breakthrough in understanding, a person's misuse of processing thinking lessens, and the time he spends in the stream increases.

With a shift in thought recognition, the range of moods that people typically experience instantly shifts upward. For example, when my level of understanding about thought broke through, so too did the overall quality of my thinking. Instantly, my "normal" feeling state shifted from stress and anxiety to a sense of ease and contentment. Immediately, life looked easier to me, full of interesting possibilities that I didn't typically see before. I began waking up into a world that appeared more intriguing and inviting. Most mornings I couldn't wait to get started. Today, the range of moods I typically experience has changed. Now, a high mood is the experience of profound gratitude and joy just for being alive. Interestingly, my lowest mood today is my old "normal" feeling state of stress and anxiety!

My former client, Jill, is another good example. For Jill, "unhappy" was her normal way of feeling for several years. Like most chronically unhappy people, the overall quality of Jill's thinking was very low. She thought primarily in the processing mode, typically entertaining thoughts about what was missing in her life. It was normal for Jill to wade knee deep in her memories about past relationships that went wrong, things she could have done if she had just gone to college, and how she was wasting her life and getting older. Jill's incessant processing thinking abuses resulted in much depression and anxiety. She felt dissatisfied and cheated by life. She was negative, pessimistic, and had little or no fun. Among other things, she coped with these painful feelings by shoplifting. This misguided activity gave her a false sense of accomplishment, as well as expensive jewelry to bolster her low self-concept.

Then, a high mood for Jill was feeling stressed and anxious which she experienced as a tremendous relief. After several therapy sessions, however, Jill's level of understanding shifted about thought and the two modes of thinking. Following this breakthrough, her typical feeling state moved from "unhappy" to feeling stressed and anxious. Soon thereafter, Jill began having moments of feeling spontaneous and playful, feelings she hadn't experienced since she was a very young child. At first, this pleasant new mood frightened her because it felt so foreign. With understanding, however, Jill saw that it was just a change in her thinking quality. Thus, she started relaxing and enjoying this "new" mood whenever it happened to occur.

Which One is the Mood?

Here's a little exercise to help you gauge your present level of understanding about moods. Please don't get serious now...it's just a game. Consider if you will the following case example. Michael is a brain surgeon who absolutely loves his work. In fact, if you asked him about it he would say that his work isn't work. He'd tell you that it's second nature to him. He'd say that he does it effortlessly...that he doesn't even have to think about it. When Michael is doing surgery, he flows. He even compares himself to a superstar athlete, making all the right moves at just the right time. In surgery, Michael experiences his moments in a full, rich way. Often, he feels exhilarated and inspired. While on the job, he experiences a sense of contribution and appreciation for life. The members of his surgical team see him as a role model and feel privileged to work with him. Michael spends about sixty to seventy hours a week at work.

At home, however, it's a whole different story. With his wife and children, Michael is a tyrant, extremely arrogant and very controlling. He has frequent angry outbursts, and often accuses his wife of not appreciating him. He has even hit her on several occasions. Also, Michael is very critical of his children. He typically focuses on what they do wrong. Compliments are rare from Michael, and generally hinge on very high levels of performance. Michael has had several extramarital affairs for which he blames his wife's weight gain. He needs at least at one martini every night to get to sleep.

Which one of these two very different versions of Michael is the mood? Is Michael's "normal" feeling state his exhilarating experience at work and his angry, negative state of mind at home the mood? Or, is Michael's lower quality experience at home "normal" for him, and his higher quality experience at work the mood? Which one do you think is a mood for Michael?

Well, you could look at it this way. Michael spends about sixty to seventy percent of his time feeling contented and satisfied at work, and only thirty to forty percent of his time feeling angry and frustrated at home. Based on percentages, one could say that Michael's experience at home is the mood. This wouldn't be the correct answer, however. Actually, Michael's "normal" feeling state is his angry, unhappy experience at home. For Michael, his work-related experience of ease and exhilaration is simply a high mood. Granted, for Michael, this mood can last for long periods of time. Nevertheless, it's just a mood.

Why is this the case for Michael? Because one's "normal" feeling state, or typical state of mind is a function of their present level of understanding or thought recognition. Michael clearly has a low level of thought recognition. He obviously has little if any awareness that he is using two completely different modes of thinking at work and at home. It's not clear to him that the mode of thinking that produces his wonderful experience at work would produce an equally high quality experience at home if he understood it and learned to access it. With understanding, Michael could begin experiencing his family as well as his work in a gratifying and exhilarating way.

Moods are Really No Big Deal

I'm certain that understanding the truth about moods will be as empowering for you as it's been for me. Through understanding, you can see that moods are really no big deal. You can recognize moods for what they really are, changes in the quality of our thinking that come and go. With a shift in understanding, you can stop fighting moods, being put off by them, and taking them so seriously. A low mood is simply one of those annoying things in life that occurs when our thinking quality drops. A high mood is just one of those more pleasant moments in life that happens when the quality of our thinking goes up. That's all that moods are. Really!

Recognizing the truth about moods will enable you to stay balanced and keep your bearings as the quality of your thinking shifts from time to time. When you clearly understand that moods are just changes in your thinking quality, you won't be confused, frightened, or deluded by them when they happen to occur. For example, when you recognize your lower moods for what they really are, it will become easy to avoid acting in misguided ways when you're experiencing the temporary reality illusions of your lower quality thinking in action. If the quality of your thinking drops, and distorted perceptions and insecure emotions are swirling around you, you can recognize what's going on, keep your bearings, and watch from the sidelines until your lower quality thought storm quiets down. When you understand the truth about moods, you can avoid becoming gripped by your lower quality thinking currents and being dragged downstream, perhaps kicking and screaming, into Fool's Creek!

Imagine how different your life could have been if you had lived in these powerful understandings back then. What foolish behaviors could you have avoided if you had understood the true nature of moods? Imagine all the feet that you wouldn't have put in your mouth!

Heck, I got married and divorced twice because I proposed and bailed out both times while I was in a lower mood. Pretty foolish...right? Yet, it was really the best I could do at the time, because my level of understanding then was quite low.

Also, I used to think that I was "just being honest," or "telling it like it really was" when I shared my lower mood viewpoints and feelings with other people. I thought that I was really contributing to people by being straight or candid with them when I was in a lower mood. Now, I realize that this behavior was pretty misguided, like having the stomach flu, throwing up on someone, and thinking I was doing them a favor!

It's likely that you, too, have your list of embarrassing, silly, foolish, even destructive things that you've done out of having little understanding about moods. Goofy, crazy, foolish, even violent behavior motivated by misunderstood, lower quality thinking episodes and the insecure emotions they spawn, results in incredible damage to people, groups, and cultures alike. When undistinguished, abuses of the processing mode, and the painful feelings and emotional highs they can spawn, account for unbelievable amounts of personal stress, devastation, and tragedy!

Diane, a client of mine, began therapy feeling extremely depressed and anxious. She had been through a series of horribly abusive relationships. While she was married, she had been so severely beaten by her husband that she ended up with mild brain damage! When she finally came to see me, Diane was in a very unhappy and troubled state of mind. In her low moods, she had flashbacks of these horribly abusive events. A particularly disturbing part of this experience was a frightening auditory hallucination, an angry voice in her head telling her how "dumb" and "stupid" she was.

During our sessions, Diane began to catch on about thought and the nature of moods. She suddenly realized that her hallucination was simply a perceptual distortion created by her basement quality thinking in action. Diane recognized that this unsettling experience was, as she put it, "thinking trash." She saw that it didn't mean that she was crazy or flawed, thoughts she had been processing and secretly believing for years.

With a shift in understanding, Diane recognized her lower mood thinking distortions for what they were. Instantly, her whole attitude and demeanor shifted. Now, when she hears "the voice," she doesn't entertain or respect it like she used to. Instead, she just thanks it for sharing, does her best to clear her mind, and waits for it to stop, which it does now much sooner.

I'll never forget the following example of low mood understanding that I heard at a POM conference in Seattle. Gordan Trockman, a POM psychiatrist, shared about one of his clients who had been diagnosed with schizophrenia. In her low moods, this client experienced a recurring visual hallucination. She would open her bathroom door and see a huge rabbit sitting on the toilet! This vision would scare the bejeebers out of her and her mood would spiral even lower.

When this woman became comfortable with Gordan, he was able, in his own way, to coach her about thought and moods. In her own way, she began to understand that "the rabbit" wasn't real, just a temporary illusion created by her low quality thinking. At a later session, it occurred to Gordan to ask her about "the rabbit." To this query she responded casually, "Oh, yes, he was there again last week when I opened the bathroom door...I just told him to hurry up and finish because I had to go."

Later in her treatment, this same client, who over the years had been seen by scads of psychiatrists, told Gordan the following, "You're the only doctor I've ever seen who wasn't afraid of me." Accurately understanding human psychological functioning also makes a big difference for the mental health of therapists! With a shift in understanding, your highest moods today can become your lowest moods tomorrow. How good can you stand it!

Chapter 12

The Real Scoop on Emotions and Higher-Order Feelings

My understanding was also way off the mark about the true nature and purpose of emotions. I realize now that I learned a slew of distorted ideas about human emotions during my training as a psychotherapist. For years, I lived my life and practiced psychotherapy actively processing these faulty beliefs about emotions. Guess what? My life and my work didn't go that well!

Take negative feelings, for example. I learned that negative emotions like depression, fear, and anger somehow added depth or substance to people's lives. I thought that experiencing such painful emotions helped people develop character and moral strength. I used to think, "You can't appreciate the good feelings in life if don't have the bad ones to compare them to."

Also, I was taught that negative emotions somehow got stored up or could accumulate in people's minds where they would silently fester, and eventually erupt or explode. I thought that people had to focus on their negative feelings and fully experience them in order to, "get them out." I believed that people had to re-live or "get in touch with" their painful, insecure emotions before they could be released. As a new therapist, my feelings motto was, "No pain...no gain!"

I can even remember searching for therapeutic techniques to re-activate people's negative emotions. I actually tried to provoke certain clients into feeling sad, angry, or guilty. You can imagine the tone of my typical therapy session. You got it...heavvvy! A session might start out light and peaceful, but I always made sure that mood didn't last very long. I'd been taught that good therapy was serious and intense. I remember a college professor who once admonished me in class, "Mr. Kelley," he bellowed, "if you're having fun in your sessions, you're not doing psychotherapy!" Thus, after perhaps a few light moments, my lower quality thinking would instruct me to "get to work." Obediently, I would change the topic or ask a question that would move things toward seriousness and more somber emotions. At the time, I genuinely believed that this approach was right and good.

During my therapy sessions, I encouraged many clients to cry, get angry, and express their other painful feelings. To me, these emotional displays meant that we were accomplishing something worthwhile and therapeutic. When a client who had cried, suffered, or grieved left my office, I secretly hoped that one of my colleagues would see his pain and think, "What good work that Kelley does!"

For many years I was the misguided prisoner of deliberately processing these biased thoughts about the nature of emotions. Today, it's hard for me to imagine that I used to glorify negative feelings and actually saw them as a way to move people toward healthier functioning. When my level of understanding was low, I couldn't see negative emotions for what they really were. Now, I finally recognize the truth about these painful feelings. Unless they're alerting us to some real physical danger like a Greyhound bus coming at us, negative emotions are <u>always</u> symptoms of lower quality processing mode habits of thinking. Negative emotions

<u>always</u> signal the fact that we're abusing the processing mode and have moved away from the stream.

That's right...negative, painful, insecure emotions won't build your character, they won't make you a better person, they won't add to your appreciation of positive feelings, they're not stored up inside of you, they can't spoil or damage you, and you don't have to "get in touch with them," or "get them out" to feel better. NON-SENSE! Dr. Roger Mills puts it this way:

> "...negative emotions are not stored up like air in a balloon or pus in an abscess; they are not forced upon us from the outside but are created moment to moment by processing mode thinking abuses. If clients realized this, they could begin to drop these low quality thinking habits that keep negative emotions in place and begin to find mental health and more loving feelings. Trying to achieve mental health via negativity is analogous to trying to achieve peace of mind through fighting. It can never be done."

Distinguishing Emotions from Higher-Order FEELINGS

Before I understood the principles of Psychology of Mind, I spent most of my life experiencing List B emotions. I realize now that my former "typical" feeling state of stress and anxiety was the product of my innocent, habitual abuse of processing thinking. These stressful emotions were simply a dance to my chronic processing of biased thoughts about how my life should be. To the degree that I saw life matching my biased expectations, I felt emotional highs like security, pride, glee, elation, arrogance, and excitement. To the extent that life failed to match these same biased thoughts, I felt painful emotions like frustration, stress, anxiety, guilt, boredom, and anger.

While the first group of so-called "positive" emotions certainly felt better than the second group of painful ones, the source of them all was exactly the same. Each of these lower quality, List B feelings, the stressful ones and the highs, was a product of misusing processing thinking. To the degree I filtered life through the biased expectations in my memory, my feelings were a mosaic of artificial highs and lows.

Occasionally, however, a curious thing would happen. Every now and then, I would experience some deeper, more profound feelings. These feelings would seem to sneak up on me. All of a sudden, I'd be in the midst of them. This experience would often happen toward the end of my Christmas and Easter trips to visit my mother, sister, and nephew in St. Pete, Florida. I would arrive at the Tampa airport feeling pretty "normal"...stressed out, and in an anxious state of mind. During the drive to St. Pete, I would usually try to impress my sister by telling her about all the "important" things I was doing back in Michigan.

For the first few days in Florida, I felt like I was going through some kind of withdrawal.   Since I didn't have my whirlwind schedule of "achievement coping activities" to perform, I would start processing thoughts like, "I should be doing something productive."   Thus, I would feel restless, on edge, and irritable. Then, perhaps on the sixth or seventh day of my usual ten-day stay, something would seem to shift. I used to think of it as a "thawing out" experience. I would notice myself melting into the moment. I would start tasting food again. I would begin seeing colors in a more deep, intense way. I would start feeling the warmth of the sun and the gentle caresses of the tropical breeze. I would become more relaxed and peaceful. I might even be moved by the magnificent beauty of the ocean and the rich, pastel sunsets. Occasionally, I'd experience a profound sense of appreciation just for being alive. I might even have deep feelings of love and gratitude for my family and friends.

At the time, I cherished these wonderful feelings but had little understanding of why or how they suddenly appeared.   I thought that I had just "mellowed out" since I was away from all that "stress" back in Detroit. At the end of these trips, I would usually have a lump of sadness in my throat. As we drove to the Tampa airport, I would be processing thoughts about going back to my same old "stressful" routine in that desolate, cold, Godforsaken town.

Now, I realize what occurred on these trips. By a certain time in my stay, my habitual processing thinking quieted down. Thus, the free-flowing mode kicked in, and I experienced a very high mood. Temporarily, I would access a higher quality group of natural feelings, higher-order human feelings that spring to life for people when they're experiencing life from the stream.

Psychology of Mind makes a very useful distinction between positive and negative emotions, and our higher-order human feelings. Emotions, whether positive or negative, are always activated by lower quality processing mode habits of thinking. List B emotional highs and lows are the only feelings possible when people are experiencing life by deliberately processing their memories. George Pransky puts it this way:

> "...Although some emotions, such as excitement, might appear to be positive, no emotions are as desirable and pleasurable as deeper human feelings. The emotion excitement as a "positive" experience, pales in comparison to the deeper feeling of exhilaration, for example. Excitement has a component of frenetic energy that needs to be maintained; exhilaration points to the inspiration of contentment and actually has a calming effect in the moment."

Processing mode - generated emotions obscure the deeper, higher-order human feelings that automatically surface when we shift into the free-flowing mode. Rich, wonderful feelings like serenity, peace of mind, genuine happiness, gratitude, wonder, appreciation, joy, intimacy, and love are available to everyone at any time. Actually, they are always just one thought away! All we have to do to release them is recognize that we're misusing our thinking, quiet our mind, and ease back into the stream.

Higher-order feelings signal high quality, free-flowing thinking in action. They signify an unconditional or non-contingent appreciation of life. This means that when people are thinking in the free-flowing mode, their enjoyment or appreciation of life isn't dependent on their circumstances.

A very healthy friend of mine shared a great example of this higher order, non-contingent enjoyment of life. It happened to her when she was working as a therapist at a psychological clinic in Michigan. One day, her clinic director invited her into his office and told her that he would like to change her job from therapist to clinic business manager. To this request my friend replied, "But, I love doing therapy!" The director quickly responded, "I know...but you love everything you do." My friend the therapist, soon to become the happy clinic business manager, thought for a moment and said, "You know something...you're right!"

Living in higher-order feelings indicates that a person is functioning at a high level of understanding, and her mind is thinking predominantly in the free-flowing mode. These universal high quality feelings are available to everyone as a way of life. They are a continuous part of the experience of higher levels of thought recognition. They are part of the package of high quality, List A experiences that all human beings were designed to live in most of the time. Dr. George Pransky puts it this way:

> "When these feelings of well-being are focused inside, they are self-esteem. When they are focused toward the future, they are hopefulness. When they are focused toward the present, they are experienced as peace of mind. When they are focused toward the past, they are experienced as gratitude. When we experience well-being in the presence of another, it is love. All these feelings are natural, desirable, and satisfying. These feelings accompany the free-flowing mode thinking continually. They are a constant manifestation of this natural way of thinking."

Emotions and FEELINGS as Thinking Quality Barometers

It's likely that you now realize the value in understanding the truth about human emotions, both negative and positive, as well as higher-order human feelings. Emotions and higher-order feelings were meant to serve as a kind of mental health barometer. Their innate purpose is to tell us the momentary quality level of our thinking.

Lower quality, artificial emotions like stress, anxiety, depression, anger, self-importance, pride, the thrill of victory, the security of life meeting our expectations, the high of getting what we want, and the glee of being right all signal lower quality processing mode habits of thinking. Higher-order feelings like natural self-worth, and non-contingent enjoyment of life signal that our mind is thinking in the free-flowing mode, and that we're operating at, or near our best.

A good illustration of understanding the true purpose of emotions and feelings happened recently to Dennis, one of my clients. Dennis was feeling peaceful and relaxed when the telephone rang. It was his good friend, Dan, who, during their conversation, told Dennis that he was making up to $450 an hour in his legal work as an expert witness. As soon as Dennis heard this, he felt some pangs of envy and fear. Dennis, however, understood that these negative, painful emotions were there to inform him that the quality of his thinking had dropped. Without this understanding, it's likely that, Dennis would have left the stream and started entertaining thoughts like, "There's something wrong with me," "I'm falling behind the pack," "I must not be as good, or successful as my friend," and "I need to work harder."

Before Dennis clearly understood the two thinking modes, and the true nature of emotions, he would have been much more likely to get suckered into a long bout with the mental flu. He would have become frightened by his insecure emotions and started reacting to them. For example, he might have ordered one of those get rich quick schemes from a late night infomercial. He might have become judgmental and looked for evidence to prove that, although his income was less, he was still more successful than Dan. He could have gotten into a fight with his wife about her spending habits.

When his level of understanding was low, Dennis would have turned up the volume of his processing thinking and become gripped by his painful thoughts in action. His mood, of course, would have spiraled downward!

Because Dennis realized the true nature of emotions, however, his perspective was different. As soon as he noticed the beginning painful feeling notes of a potential mental flu symphony, he automatically knew what would happen if he started deliberately squeezing the painful thoughts that were conducting the orchestra. With understanding, instead of adding the strings, brass, horns, cymbals, and drums to a potential low quality thinking serenade, and risking full-blown mental pneumonia, Dennis didn't entertain them. He realized that his feeling was off, and he didn't act. From his new level of understanding, Dennis remained secure and responsive, and stayed in the stream.

Dennis told me that later that day, he actually experienced feelings of gratitude and appreciation for his friend's success and achievements. These higher-order feelings would not have been possible for Dennis before he caught on to the principles of POM, including the true nature and purpose of emotions and higher-order feelings.

Just like physical pain tells us that something's wrong with us physically, the role of emotions, whether positive or negative, is to alert us that our thinking quality is low. Higher-order List A feelings like optimism, joy, well-being, peace of mind, and natural happiness let us know that our thinking is free-flowing, and that our level of mental functioning is high quality. The purpose of these natural feelings is to let us know that we're heading in the right direction, and that whatever we have to do, we're in a good state of mind to do it. Higher-order feelings are a green light to inform us that it's safe to proceed on course. They let us know that we're operating at or close to our best.

When viewed from this new perspective, emotions and deeper human feelings become faithful guides to living in the neighborhood of List A as a way of life. They will always tell us when to slow down and quiet our mind. They will warn us when we are literally an accident waiting to happen. They will faithfully tell us when we're in a spinning-our-wheels-but-not-going-anywhere level of functioning. Again, in the words of Dr. Roger Mills:

"...as we begin to understand the real significance behind what we feel, we begin to realize that emotions and Feelings are an internal compass that can guide us past the pitfalls in life, regardless of the details or conditions that exist around us. Good feelings (higher-order ones) let us know that our thinking is of higher quality and that we are moving in the right direction. If we feel negative, hostile, or depressed, it's time to step back and relax, to suspend struggle and judgments. If we wait patiently and quiet our mind, the common sense of wisdom will shine through the clouds and our thinking will be healthy once again."

How good can you stand it!

Chapter 13

Now What? Deepening Your Level of Understanding - Part I

N ow you have all of the pieces to the puzzle of human psychological functioning! Now you know exactly how all human beings work psychologically in each and every moment. The three principles and core concepts of Psychology of Mind explain every state of mind that you've ever experienced. They make sense of every emotion you've ever felt. They make clear every behavior that you've ever done.

From your new level of understanding, you can now plant your hands securely on the steering wheel of your psychological functioning. Now, you have the thought recognition necessary to allow your natural, free-flowing thinking to effortlessly steer you toward more genuine happiness and contentment. Now you can recognize and respond more sensibly when the quality of your thinking shifts along the way.

The "Now what?" question in this chapter title is a trick one. It suggests that now that you've moved to a new level of thought recognition, there's something that you need to do with this shift in understanding.   The truth, of course, is that there's absolutely nothing to do! You don't have to <u>do</u> anything with a true shift in understanding. Through a breakthrough in understanding alone, the time you'll spend in free-flowing thinking will automatically grow, without any effort from you.

In this chapter, I'd like to share with you some additional slices of the powerful principles of POM. It's my intention that these different views move you to an even deeper level of understanding about the role of thought in creating your on-going life experience. It might be helpful to view the topics that we'll explore as pieces of effortless, thought recognition deepening, Nautilus equipment.   You can reflect on each topic with the intention of moving to an even deeper, more profound level of thought recognition. In our breakthrough gymnasium, all you have to do is quiet your mind and see what occurs to you as we visit each station.

Again, this isn't about learning some POM tips or techniques. This isn't coaching about a formula or recipe for getting better. All you have to do is clear your mind and continue to listen for <u>not</u> knowing. Remember, if you let the stream listen for you, your present level of understanding will be much more likely to leap forward. Shifts in understanding, not tips or techniques, are all that matter. No pain...all gain!

Experiencing Your True Self as a Way of Life

Now you know that who you truly are is a human being with the divine gift of thought designed to work effortlessly in a free-flowing way. Your mind's natural design to keep you primarily in the intelligent stream of responsive, gliding thought is always poised to do so. It might be helpful to compare your innate blueprint to think predominantly in the free-flowing mode to a cork floating in a pool of water. Misusing your processing thinking acts like a weight pushing down on the cork. The lower your mood, the heavier the weight of misused processing thinking pushing down on the buoyant, natural source of your innate, healthy functioning.

Free-flowing thinking is always ready to bob up high above the surface of the water as soon as the misused processing thinking weight is removed from the cork.

Remember, at least to some degree we all have innocently learned to misuse processing thinking. One unfortunate result was the activation of identity illusions like "ego" and "self-image," or who we really aren't. From your new level of thought recognition, you can now see the paradox of these false or artificial identities. Those times in your life when you've experienced higher-order feelings and performed effortlessly, at or close to your best? Those were the times that you stopped deliberately living life through the self-evaluation thoughts in your memory, and these "pain magnet" identity illusions momentarily dissolved. During those periods of "temporary sanity," your mind cleared, and you accessed your natural free-flowing thinking. Thus, at least for a while, your ego illusion vanished, and you experienced the real you.

When your level of understanding was low, however, it's likely that these wonderful reunions with your true self were more random and short-lived. Before your thought recognition shifted upward, it's likely that your natural mental health cork got weighed down by misused processing thinking habits more often, more heavily, and much longer than necessary.

Please let me share another example from my past. It was a time when, at least in one area of my life, I inadvertently stopped trying to prove my worth, and my habitual processing thinking temporarily quieted down. For a while, I started being my true self as my lower quality thinking weight fell off the cork, and my free-flowing thinking kicked in. Unfortunately, I didn't have the thought recognition then to realize what transpired.

It happened back in college. I was a member of a social fraternity called Delta Chi. By that time, I had become an expert at misusing the processing mode. I had designed a huge "ego illusion" that looked very real to me. The thoughts in action that sustained this illusion had me see my fraternity, like they had me see most areas of my life, as a place to prove that I was special and important. Therefore, it shouldn't surprise you that I decided to run for fraternity president. Of course I did, and guess what? In a close race, I lost.

When I learned the election results, I started processing in high gear. I became livid. I blamed my defeat on some slanderous remarks that a few brothers in the other camp had spread. My "ego illusion" screamed with a vengeance. "To heck with them!" it bellowed, "If they don't want me as their president, from now on I'm not going to do any official work in this fraternity...no committees, no meetings, no duties, nothing!"

I had no idea then that it was my lower quality thinking deciding me. At the time, it really appeared to me that I was right and justified in this decision. To prove it, I went around and collected plenty of "agreement thoughts" from other members of the group.

Following this decision, however, an interesting thing began to happen. Since my way of coping with losing the election was to withhold participation, I didn't have to prove myself by participating anymore. Thus, my deliberate processing thinking, at least in the realm of formal fraternity activities, quieted down significantly. Lo and behold, with less low quality thought weight on my mental health cork, more moments of free-flowing thinking surfaced. Thus, at least in the realm of fraternity, I relaxed, felt more spontaneous, and actually began having some genuine fun!

I had no idea then what had occurred. I just experienced more contentment and happiness that year I lost the election than any other year in college. Since I was inadvertently being my true self more often, I made new friends and became better liked by my fraternity brothers than ever before.

If only I had understood what happened. My thought recognition then was pretty low, however, and my lower quality thinking habits were waiting eagerly in the background, ready to pounce. The opportunity soon came. You got it...the next election for fraternity officers was right around the corner. Better-liked than ever before, I again ran for president. This time, however, I won easily. Hello, processing mode...good-bye, true self. Down went my mental health cork. As fraternity president, my percentage of misused processing thinking skyrocketed and my level of satisfaction and happiness diminished proportionately!

Now, please don't get me wrong. There's nothing bad or wrong about achievement or accomplishment. There's nothing inherently stressful about actively participating in the game of life. The problem shows up when people learn to play the game while chronically misusing their processing thinking, and innocently lose themselves in the process. From the lower quality perspectives brought to life by misusing Mode Two, the game of life can look pretty intense and serious. Often, people innocently start confusing themselves with the roles that they're playing in the game. Then, fraternity president wasn't just a role I was assuming. It was who I thought I really was! My accomplishments back then were motivated more by lower quality List B emotions like the fear of failure and the excitement of winning. Seldom, did I experience higher-order feelings like gratitude, commitment, and the desire to serve that show up when people are simply being themselves, human beings thinking effortlessly, in a free-flowing way.

From your new level of understanding, you can now see the joke of "ego" and "self-image." Now, you can see the futility in trying to move into List A by strengthening or working on these identity illusion pain magnets. To build up your "ego," or improve your "self-image," you have to sacrifice the real you. You have to continue misusing Mode Two - processing thinking, and pile up the weight on your free-flowing cork!

I remember how it was for me when I first realized what fueling my processing mode generated artificial identities was costing me in missed List A healthy functioning. When my level of understanding shifted, I instantly saw many new behaviors that made perfect sense. For example, at parties I stopped bragging to people about my recent accomplishments. I stopped automatically telling people who didn't know me that I was <u>Dr.</u> Kelley. Instead, I started introducing myself as Tom Kelley. Also, I began asking people more questions about themselves. I started listening more intently to people, instead of figuring out the next thing that I was going to say. I spent more time with the female guests because their conversations were less likely to trigger my lower quality thinking habits.

From my new level of understanding, these new behaviors didn't take effort, they weren't techniques, they just made sense. Instantly, I began experiencing my social activities in an entirely different way. I actually started relaxing, having fun, enjoying myself, and feeling genuinely liked by people. For the first time, I had the wondrous experience of partying from the stream!

When people have a low level of understanding, it often appears to them that processing mode thinking misuses like worrying, finding fault, defending their views, trying to change things out there, playing the "more, better, different game," and running their "ego" acts, are sensible things to do. With a shift in understanding, however, it occurs to people that each of these lower quality thinking habits, and the coping mechanisms they spawn only keeps them out of the stream. The deeper your level of understanding, the more you'll automatically stay in the stream and enjoy the natural experience of being your true self as a way of life.

The Illusion of Problems, Needs, and Urges

From your new level of understanding, it may have already occurred to you that problems, needs, and urges are all illusions brought to life by the misuse of processing thinking. There are no such entities as problems, needs, or urges. Each is an apparition that can be experienced as real by people, when they're misusing the processing mode, and have a low level of thought recognition.

Please think about it...when you're deliberately "squeezing" painful thoughts or memories, life can appear negative, overwhelming, and unmanageable. When we're misusing Mode Two, just about anything can seem like a problem. For example, depending on the thoughts I'm holding in my mind, my house can look like an old money pit that needs all kinds of costly renovation, my students can appear less intelligent, even boring, and my writing can become awkward and labored. However, as soon as I relax, clear my mind, and ease into free-flowing thinking once again, everything shifts. Suddenly, I have this quaint, charming house, my students become brighter and more interesting, and my writing starts flowing and becomes more satisfying once again.

Problems disappear when our thinking is free-flowing. In the stream, problems are transformed. When our thinking is flowing freely, life's challenges seem not only more manageable, but often appear as intriguing opportunities. When people stop deliberately processing their "problem thoughts," they're not in denial...they're just disengaging the processing thinking misuse that has "problem mirages" appear in the first place.

Needs, like problems, are solely a lower quality thinking phenomenon. Unfortunately, we live in a low quality thinking culture, a culture in which it's "normal" to overuse and misuse the processing mode. Therefore, it's not surprising that so many people typically dwell on thoughts like, "I must have my needs satisfied to be happy."

When they're living outside of the stream, people often do feel needy and dependent. Why? Because many people have learned to habitually process thoughts that tie their worth or security to things out there...thoughts that their well-being hinges on their family and friends meeting their "love needs"...their employer supplying their "security needs"...and the government giving them what think they're entitled to have.

With little thought recognition, many people spend much of their time trying to manipulate people and circumstances in misguided attempts to "get their needs met." Even many well-intentioned therapists support their clients in this self-defeating, disempowering vicious circle.

The joke is that when people's thinking is free-flowing, needs (except for food, water, and shelter) don't even exist. When the free-flowing mode is at the helm, people feel satisfied and fulfilled no matter what the circumstances in their lives. From the stream, people may see things they <u>want</u>, but they don't have the experience of needing them.

With a shift in level of understanding, people gain an entirely new perspective on needs. They let the "need satisfiers" in their life off the hook. They see the painful feelings of neediness and dependency for what they really are...symptoms of Mode Two thinking misuse. They stop the vicious circle of misusing processing thinking, feeling needy and dependent, struggling to get their "needs" met, and blaming someone (including themselves) or some entity ("the system") if they aren't. The mirage of needs, and the feelings of dependency that go with them appear less often as people start trusting their free-flowing thinking. With Mode One at the helm, people automatically feel more fulfilled and self-sufficient no matter what's going on around them.

You've got it...it works exactly the same way with urges. Urges are simply another List B outcome of misusing the processing mode to "squeeze" painful thoughts connected with certain misguided coping behaviors. It's helpful to remember that all bad habits like smoking, overeating, gambling, worrying, and violence, are people's way of coping with the painful emotions they typically experience when they live chronically outside of the stream.

When people's level of understanding deepens, however, they see that they were never "bad" or "sick" because they had, and often gave in to their "urges." They recognize that this misguided behavior was truly the best way they could see at the time to calm the painful products of their unrecognized processing thinking abuses. As people allow the free-flowing mode to become the conductor of their thinking, their problem, need, and urge illusions automatically quiet and even disappear. How good can you stand it!

Chapter 14

Deepening Your Level of Understanding - Part II

Dealing With "Difficult" People

Dealing with "difficult" people is thought to be one of the biggest sources of stress in our culture. Why is it so hard for most people to keep their balance when they encounter "difficult" people? When these so-called "difficult" individuals get angry at us, treat us with little respect or concern, ignore us, or do some other rude or nasty thing in our presence, why do we tend to get so bent out of shape?

For one thing, most people don't understand the misguided behavior of "difficult" people. Most people don't realize the true significance of "difficult" behavior in all of its many forms and variations. Often, this misunderstanding has people react to such behavior in a personal way. They misguidedly interpret it as a slap at their personal worth or dignity. They think that if they don't stand up to "difficult" people they risk being conned or perceived as a "doormat" or "wimp!"

A whole industry of seminars, courses, tapes, and books has evolved to teach us how to deal with "difficult" people. Many of these products promote the idea that we have a right to be hurt or angry when such people treat us badly. Most propose that we learn to express our painful feelings to these "bullies" in assertive ways. Some even suggest that we retaliate against "difficult" people by ignoring them, withholding our affection, leaving them, or even treating them the same way they're treating us. Millions of people have learned these coping techniques. Yet, all too often, they continue to feel distressed about "difficult" people.

From your new level of understanding, dealing with "difficult" people will naturally become much easier. Why? Because when people finally get clear about human psychological functioning, they realize the truth about chronically "difficult" individuals. They see that such people are almost continually gripped by their low quality processing mode thinking habits. "Difficult" people chronically misuse processing thinking. They typically view life through biased, painful memories and experience insecure feelings and distorted perceptions. Their so-called "difficult behavior," in all of its forms, is simply the best way they can see to cope with the lower quality, List B view of life in which they typically reside.

When people understand the principles of POM, they get clear that the misguided behavior of "difficult" people never means anything personal. Other than the fact that you may be in one of their lower quality processing spotlights on a particular day, their behavior has no bearing at all on your worth or value as a person. It may look personal to your "ego" and "self-image" illusions, but in fact, it never is.

How, then, should you deal with "difficult" people? What if you have one for a boss? What if you happen to be married to one? What if one is your child or parent? Well, you'll just have to trust your high quality, free-flowing thinking to show you a way that makes the most sense in each situation. When you're living in the stream, you won't experience someone's "difficult" behavior in a personal way. You'll view it with more understanding, perspective, even compassion. Also, you'll access more sensible, even creative responses.

Depending on the situation, I've responded to "difficult" people by being assertive, passive, aggressive, humble, making them right, ignoring them, agreeing with them, reassuring them, staying away from them, firing them, having them arrested, getting to know them, and loving them exactly the way they are. From the stream, each of these varied responses made sense to me at one time or another. When my thinking is free-flowing, I can count on my natural intuition and common sense to guide me. If my thinking quality drops, and it starts to look personal, I do my best to quiet my mind and not react.

When people clearly understand human psychological functioning, they naturally stop worrying once and for all about how people might treat them. Why? Because they recognize that it's never personal, and that their well-being isn't in the hands of others. Also, they begin to experience compassion for people who are hurting. Of course, they still take care of themselves, and get out of the way when it makes sense to do so.

When people are operating from the stream, they have more perspective and can see that in each moment, a person is in the state of mind he's in, with the level of understanding he has. That's the simple truth for all human beings. When people clearly recognize this basic psychological fact, they lighten up and become empowered to do what makes the most sense with all people, "difficult," or otherwise.

The Illusion of Traumatization and Permanent Damage

Another myth perpetuated by an inaccurate understanding of human psychological functioning is that people can be permanently damaged or traumatized by certain horrific events. I teach a course on child abuse and neglect at the University. Each year as I prepare for this class, I find articles written by experts in the field proclaiming that children who are severely abused are destined to become "damaged goods." By this they mean that most abused children are hopelessly doomed to be depressed, afraid, and angry for the rest of their lives. Many people believe that these "damaged" youngsters can never experience trusting, intimate relationships with other people. Furthermore, as adults they must constantly be on guard, lest they abuse their own children.

Of course, terrible things do happen to people, often through no fault of their own. It's a shame that so many people have to experience hideous, often random acts of violence and destruction. It's essential that each of us do whatever we can to prevent such horrible acts from occurring. It's important to extend support and compassion to people who experience such awful situations.

In the meantime, it's very helpful for people to see that what psychologists call "emotional scars" are simply memories that get etched into people's minds. These memories have absolutely no power when understood for what they are and left alone. When people begin deliberately "squeezing" these painful memories, however, they will re-experience the original disturbing feelings and frightening perceptions.

It's helpful to remember that emotions don't get stored in memory, only thoughts! It's always misusing the processing mode to hold painful memories in place that sustains painful feelings in the present. In the free-flowing mode, these exact same painful memories will always be experienced with more perspective and wisdom. With a shift in understanding, people can see how misusing Mode Two thinking brings these horrible past moments back to life. With a shift in thought recognition, people can stop camping out with their painful memories when they come floating down the stream.

I once heard a powerful true story about a very high functioning woman who was raped, beaten, and left on the side of the road to die. Another man came by and saw her. To her horror, this would-be Samaritan also raped her and shot her in the head! Sometime later, still clinging to life, she was discovered and rushed to the hospital. She eventually recovered, but was totally blinded by the gunshot wound!

About two months after this horrible incident, the woman was recuperating in her hospital room. A visitor, sitting at her side, was livid, seething with anger about what had happened to her friend. The "victim," however, was exceedingly calm, content, and very optimistic about her future. This healthy perspective upset her visitor even more. "How can you be so calm about this?" she shrieked, "If this had happened to me I'd be bitter for the rest of my life." To this, the woman replied compassionately, "I know how much you care, but I see it this way. I gave those two men thirty minutes of my life. I'm not going to give them one second more!"

Roger Mills, in his ground-breaking book, *Realizing Mental Health*, talks about receiving a federal grant to implement a county-wide training program for agencies working with high-risk, dysfunctional families. Many of the children in these families had been battered or sexually abused. Roger points out that before his program, these agencies had led many of the children to believe that their hideous experiences had damaged them in irreversible ways. After coaching these youngsters about the principles of Psychology of Mind, Roger notes the following:

> "By showing the children how they were misusing their thinking to carry their traumas close to the heart, they were able to wedge a distance between themselves and their terrible memories. They learned to keep the past from infecting the present without denying the horror that occurred. The improvement they showed - in their attitudes, their relationships with their parents, their schoolwork, and every other aspect of their lives - was remarkable. When people learn how their thinking works - and thus, how to nip their lower quality thinking in the bud - then they begin taking control of their lives, not re-living their traumas."

Transforming the Experience of Change

I'm writing this section of the book in late December. This time of year, the media is constantly running features about people's New Year's resolutions. Every year around this time, millions of people resolve to change themselves in a myriad of ways...their weight, smoking, nutrition, exercise, job, education, relationships, self-worth, stress, and on and on. By March, most will have given up. Many will be left with a slew of broken promises and feelings of failure and discouragement. Others will work their fannies off and, at least for a while, fulfill many of their resolutions. Yet, even for most of these "successful" people, their "change" experience will be effortful, a struggle, even drudgery!

Why does this "resolution ritual" repeat itself year after year? Because for far too many people, the desire to change comes mainly from lower quality processing mode habits of thinking and the identity illusions they spawn like "ego" and "self-image." Many people in our culture have learned to habitually process thoughts that they "should" or "must" change to improve their self-worth. When people don't recognize this as a misuse of Mode Two thinking, they tend to become gripped by the illusion that the way they are isn't good enough. Thus, for many people, the urge to change is motivated primarily by List B emotions like fear, guilt, pride, excitement, and anger.

Now, you can see why trying to change in order to get better never really works. Even if people do achieve their goals, change motivated by misused Mode Two thinking is hard, a struggle, burdensome.   That's   why   so   many   well-intentioned   people eventually give up. That's why the same people often make the same resolutions, New Year after New Year.

From your new level of understanding, you now recognize that high quality thinking, not change, is always the answer. When people move back to the stream, they automatically find healthier states of mind in which the motivations du jour include wisdom, natural self-esteem, inspiration, and joy. From the more sensible perspectives of free-flowing thinking, people can see more clearly what makes sense for them to change, and how to do it in more wise, satisfying ways.

When people's thinking is free-flowing, they always feel more complete and satisfied just the way they are, and they may choose to change something.   Believe me, this is an entirely different experience of change.   When we're thinking in the free-flowing mode, the <u>process</u> of change is effortless, satisfying, and enlivening.   From the stream, the results of change become secondary to savoring the journey.

The Possibility of Stress Elimination

We have loads of misguided ideas about stress in this culture. For one thing, most people believe that if you're out there actively participating in life, stress is inevitable. Most people think, "Life is tough and along with the good comes the stress."   The prominent idea that people have to learn how to cope with life is based on the assumption that life is indeed stressful. Retirement is supposedly that wonderful time in life when people get rid of most of their stress and finally start living. Yet, many large companies regularly conduct seminars on coping with retirement stress!

Also, most people believe that the source or cause of stress is somewhere out there, in external circumstances, events, and people. There's work stress caused by job duties and supervisors, relationship stress caused by partners and children, holiday stress caused by shopping and partying, and post-traumatic stress disorder caused by traumatic events. The list of stressors gets longer every year. A recent addition is seasonal affective disorder (SAD), or stress caused by the weather!

It's as if there were all these little stress particles out there attached to various things. If you get too close to them, you catch it. Zap...you're stressed!   Psychologists have even invented stress scales on which you get a certain number of stress points for enduring particular life events like a move, a job change, a new mortgage, or a divorce. The more stress points you accumulate, the more likely it is that you'll get physically sick or experience an accident in the near future. Most people have innocently learned to process these misguided thoughts about stress.   Thus, most mornings they wake up to a "stressful" world.

From your new understanding vantage point, you can now see that the real cause of the experience of stress is always the abuse of the processing mode.   When people don't realize that the experience of chronic stress, or "burnout" is their feelings smoke alarm trying to alert them that they're living chronically outside the stream, they will naively conclude that it was life that did them in.

Any time we deliberately move out of the stream, life becomes stressful.   Ironically, even many well-intentioned psychotherapists misguidedly try to help their "stressed" clients by using techniques that encourage them to abuse their processing thinking. Allan Flood puts it this way:

> "Living in that flowing stream of natural, responsive, gliding thinking gives us the life we want - fulfilling, satisfying. Anything that takes us out of the stream gives us headaches (physical and emotional). Focusing on our memories takes us out of the stream. Analyzing our problems takes us out of the stream. Getting into our negative emotions (catharsis) takes us out of the stream.   Freud (and most psychological approaches that I know about, except for Psychology of Mind) advocate one or more of these techniques for becoming healthier.   These techniques are, literally, symptoms of mental dysfunction rather than ways to get better."

It's helpful to see that there is no such thing as stress out there! Life isn't stressful. Your mother-in-law isn't stressful. Your clients aren't stressful.   Your boss isn't stressful.   Winter isn't stressful. Even a bad hair day isn't stressful. There are no stressors out there. Yes, bad things do happen to people that certainly aren't their fault.   Yet, people's experience of every event is always determined by the momentary quality of their thinking.

There is only stressful thinking and it's not happening out there. The experience of stress is always produced from the inside-out. From your new understanding vantage point, you now realize how to access the natural, free-flowing source of a stress free life.

Putting the Past in the Past and Allowing the Future to Unfold

When people understand the principles of Psychology of Mind, they become clear that the past and the future are ideas that exist only in thought. All we ever really have is the present or successive moments of now. Each of us always lives in the moment. We have absolutely no choice about that. We do have a choice, however, about how we experience our present moments. We can misuse the processing mode and live in the bland, anemic, plastic, redundant, stressful, agitated, frightening, even tormenting moments spawned by our memories in action, or we can live in the rich, vivid, satisfying, inspiring, exhilarating moments guided by the wise, intelligent stream of free-flowing thought.

When people trust and ease into free-flowing thinking, their present moments unfold in a rich, fulfilling, satisfying manner. It's not that such people aren't organized or responsible. It's not that they go off to the beach and do whatever they want. People who live primarily in the stream are generally well-organized and highly responsible. Thinking mainly in a free-flowing way, such people realize that they don't need set formulas or fixed recipes to plan for the future. Fixed formulas and set plans for designing futures are products of misused processing thinking...more tools to cope with the illusion of an "unpredictable" life. Living life in the stream is the natural source of the spontaneous unfolding of high quality future moments of now.

The misguided habits of "dwelling on," "living in," and "blaming the past" represent still other misuses of the processing mode. When a person is living in, dwelling on, or having trouble "letting go" of the past, she is misusing Mode Two...innocently gripped by her biased memories in action. Such people misguidedly spend much of their time re-thinking thoughts like, "It was better then," or "I'll never be as happy as I was in the good old days," or "My mother loved my brother more than me," or "I'll never forgive my father for abandoning me."

When people clearly understand human psychological functioning, it makes perfect sense to them to stop making themselves and other people wrong for past actions. Why?

Because they get real clear that <u>everyone always does the best they can</u> given the momentary quality of their thinking, and their present level of understanding.   With thought recognition, people realize that at any moment in time, human behavior is a dance perfectly correlated with the quality of people's thinking. This psychological fact is true for you, your parents, your wife, your boss, your friends, your children, your in-laws...all of them.   In each moment, we all dance the dance of our own thinking quality and most people don't know it.   In fact, most people don't know that they don't know!

Now, however, <u>you do know!</u>   From your new level of understanding, it makes perfect sense to let yourself and other people off the hook about the past.   With a shift in understanding, people naturally stop blaming others, and themselves, for how their lives have turned out.   With a shift in thought recognition, people instantly see the futility of dwelling on, or reliving the past, in order to get better in the present.

The past as a "problem" exists only when both the quality of our thinking and the level of our understanding are low.   When our thinking is free-flowing, we automatically access the natural, healing, flowing salve of wisdom, forgiveness, and compassion. With a shift in understanding, people can put the past back where it belongs...in the past.   Then they can sit back and relax in the natural stream of intelligent, responsive, gliding thought, and watch with exhilaration and joy as their future naturally unfolds.   How good can you stand it!

Chapter 15

When We All Understand - Unleashing the Human Potential

O ne wondrous outcome of experiencing a true breakthrough in understanding is "vision." Once people shift to a totally new perspective, they begin to foresee future possibilities that they could never before imagine. This experience is called "vision."

Psychology of Mind has provided us with a powerful new vantage point from which to view the human potential. Once people experience this new paradigm, once they realize the power and accuracy of this health unleashing model, their relationship with their psychological functioning is forever transformed. Once people saw for themselves that the world was round, going back to a flat world view was impossible.

As with any scientific breakthrough, some people catch on before others. Very quickly, those first "understanders" experience vision. Webster defines vision as, "an unusual ability in foreseeing what's going to happen." When people shift to a new level of understanding, they begin to foresee future possibilities that others cannot yet comprehend.

This chapter is an invitation to envision that future. Now that you've experienced a breakthrough in understanding regarding our human birthright of healthy psychological functioning, I'd like to request your company on a journey of foresight and imagination. Please join me in foreseeing what the world will be like when most everyone understands.

When most people have experienced the breakthrough principles of Psychology of Mind, extraordinary shifts will occur in virtually every social realm. There will be profound transformations in human relationships, social problems like crime and delinquency, the media, organizations and businesses, psychodiagnostics and psychotherapy, education, politics and government, and international relations. Please join me in envisioning the possibilities inherent in our limitless human potential. Help me illuminate the vision of **a world that works for everyone**!

Relationships

Let's begin our journey in the domain of relationships. This is a perfect starting point because relationships are the building blocks of all social endeavors. The quality of our ability to relate to one another determines how marriages work, how families function, how organizations operate, how politics and government unfold, what the media depicts, and how countries interact. At the core of every social process is relationships. How human beings relate to one another determines the quality of life on the entire planet!

How will the nature of relationships shift when most everyone understands the principles and core concepts of Psychology of Mind? Let's use the principle of Thought from which to envision this possibility. What if everyone understood and typically behaved in accordance with the simple fact that everyone experiences life through their thoughts in action? What if we all recognized the simple fact that our moment to moment reality is always created through thought, and that because no two people have exactly the same thoughts, everyone sees things differently? What if we all lived from this understanding, and were as clear about it as we are that the world is round?

Assuming this shared level of understanding about the principle of Thought, what shift would occur in the arena of relationships? I've presented my vision below. Please feel free to add any other possibilities that you foresee.

Question: What would it mean for relationships if everyone deeply understood the principle of Thought?

Possibility: The fact that each person sees life differently would be accepted by people as a simple truth.

Question: What difference would <u>that</u> make for relationships?

Possibility: The fact that everyone sees things differently would stop showing up as threatening to people. Instead, it would be seen as an interesting, even fascinating phenomenon.

Question: What difference would <u>that</u> make for relationships?

Possibility: People would be much less likely to fight with one another in order to prove that their personal reality illusions were the right or the truth.

Question: What difference would <u>that</u> make for relationships?

Possibility: People would stop relating to each other through processing mode-generated identity illusions like "ego" and "self-image." They would take their momentary personal realities much less seriously.

Question: What difference would <u>that</u> make?

Possibility: With heightened thought recognition, people would typically relate to each other from the healthier perspectives of free-flowing thinking.

Question: What difference would <u>that</u> make?

Possibility: Thinking predominantly in the free-flowing mode, people would experience more sustained, positive, higher-order feelings and tend to bring out the best in each other.

Question: What difference would <u>that</u> make?

Possibility: Typical relationships would be more intimate, creative, productive, wise, cooperative, flexible, trustworthy, patient, generous, compassionate, and appreciative.

Question: What difference would <u>that</u> make?

Possibility: People would start working together in more cooperative, common sense ways to find solutions and answers to problems in all areas of life (poverty, crime, hunger, etc.). Ending such negative social conditions in the world would become an idea whose time has come!

Question: What difference would <u>that </u>make?

Possibility: _____

                 _____

                 _____

Please fill in your vision.

Social Problems Like Crime and Delinquency

Recently, Bud, a university colleague of mine, requested my opinion about some behavior that he'd observed and couldn't quite understand. Bud was doing survey research on juvenile gangs in Detroit. As part of his study, he was interviewing several young gang members. One of these was a 14-year-old adolescent from the most crime-infested area of the city. He was a member of probably the most violent youth gang in Detroit. To call him "tough" would be an understatement. In fact, according to Bud, this 14-year-old "kid" had admitted shooting at least three people!

After an interview session with this youngster, Bud spontaneously asked him if he had ever been to the Detroit Zoo. When the youth said "No," Bud invited him to go there with he and his family. To Bud's surprise, the youth accepted!

On the following Sunday afternoon, Bud, his wife, and their two young children met this youth at a fast food restaurant in his neighborhood. During their drive to the zoo, about 20 minutes away, the boy was heavily engaged in his macho, gangster "ego" act. According to Bud, "You could see it in his walk, his mannerisms, his voice, and his language. In every pore of his being was this tough guy bravado. Actually, it was quite disturbing to all of us. For a while, I wondered if I'd made a big mistake by inviting him."

It was after they arrived at the zoo and started observing the animals that the phenomenon occurred that Bud was trying to understand. According to Bud, "Almost like magic, this tough, gangster-like kid started transforming into a typical 14-year-old adolescent!" Bud said that in minutes, his voice changed from a deep macho tone to a more mellow, natural pitch. His gait shifted from a "swagger" to a more normal walk. His body relaxed, and his defensive grimace faded away. He even cracked an occasional smile, and began relating to Bud's children in a slightly affectionate manner. Bud exclaimed, "The kid went from Mr. Hyde to Dr. Jekyll in virtually no time flat!"

Bud went on to report that this shift in behavior lasted much of the day. Occasionally, the youngster would slip back slightly, like when he walked past a group of teenage boys. Yet, for the most part, the metamorphosis persisted until later that day when they were back in the car approaching the boy's neighborhood. Bud said that during the drive home, the youth gradually shifted back to his gangster persona. As he walked from the car with a cool swagger and a "thumbs up" gesture of acknowledgment, the reverse transformation was complete.

Bud's story is a poignant illustration of the inner core of healthy psychological functioning that exists underneath the low quality processing mode thinking habits of even the most chronic, hard core delinquent juveniles. When the youth in this story was away from his dangerous environment with an accepting, non-threatening family, and absorbed in a totally new activity, he became distracted from his processing mode created violent identity illusion. Instantly, he shifted into free-flowing thinking. The result..."temporary sanity"...a short visit to List A!

When criminal justice personnel catch on to the principles of Psychology of Mind, there will be a major shift in understanding about the etiology of delinquent and criminal behavior. It will be recognized that most offenders have an inherent and natural capacity to function in more mature, common sense, non-criminal ways. It will be understood that this natural ability to access healthy functioning is often severely short-circuited because offenders function at more insecure levels due to the kinds of dysfunctional processing mode thinking habits they've learned.

Once the criminal justice field experiences this shift in understanding, its approach to the prevention and treatment of delinquent behavior will transform. With heightened thought recognition, the field will help offenders realize what insecurity is, where it comes from, and how to avoid it. Soon, offenders will recognize the true source of their painful feelings. As their level of understanding shifts, they will begin to free themselves from the grip of processing mode thinking abuses that have kept their anti-social coping actions in place.

As teachers, probation officers, police officers, and parents understand these principles, they will learn to distinguish the quality of their own thinking and significantly change their patterns of interacting with at-risk youth in a more positive direction. They will stop reacting to the "difficult" behavior of these youngsters, and begin to intervene with more common sense, positive approaches. Soon, more of the natural health of these misguided children will begin to rise to the surface.

The vision is materializing. Intervention projects using the principles of Psychology of Mind have already been implemented in some of the most crime-infested inner city housing projects in Florida, California, New York, Minnesota, and Hawaii. Testing before and after these programs has revealed that the majority of at-risk youth involved, significantly changed their outlook, expectations, and behavior. Levels of conflict dropped dramatically in 87% of families tested. Grade point averages of at-risk students improved by 65%. Self-esteem scores rose from the 40th to the 80th percentile. Absenteeism and school discipline referrals dropped below national averages. Teen pregnancy rates plummeted!

As the teenagers in these programs began to recognize their common functioning, they saw the unnecessary turmoil they were causing themselves by emphasizing their differences. They realized how their lower quality thinking habits stopped them from appreciating each other. Soon, they began to forge solid friendships across races and cultures.

When most of us catch on to these powerful principles, we will see that the challenge of ending crime and delinquency is not in trying to fix something in offenders that is missing or damaged. We will see, instead, that the real quest is to rekindle what is already within, to draw out those inherent qualities of heart and spirit that are available to all youth in each and every moment.

The Media

When people realize the principles of Psychology of Mind, they begin to see that many of the prominent themes in today's popular media are a reflection of the lower quality thinking habits of our culture.   Major media themes like sexual exploitation, violence, and deceit reflect the habitual abuse of processing thinking in our culture and the insecure feelings, distorted perceptions, and dysfunctional coping behaviors it spawns.

Today, the most popular themes in our contemporary media are clearly a reflection of our infamous List B. It's not surprising, that a culture that's learned to see stress, problems, needs, urges, conflict, ruthless competition, and aggression as "normal," even healthy functioning would be drawn to List B media products. It's no revelation, that people who are often stuck in insecure states of mind would crave violent, sensational, emotionally wrenching media events as a distraction from the noise of their lower quality thinking. It's no surprise, that a culture that has innocently learned to habitually process useless thought programs, like self-worth being tied to externals, would be enamored with affluent movie stars, sitcom celebrities, and superstar athletes, often big on "looking good," and small on healthy functioning.

When more people catch on to the principles of Psychology of Mind, they will become disenchanted with the products of our current media. Their desire for media highs to look good, feel better, or "be right" will naturally diminish. They will become less attracted to List B themes of violence, righteousness, and negativity.

When people start thinking primarily in the free-flowing mode, more mature, wise, and compassionate tastes will automatically be awakened. People will naturally be drawn to and request very different media themes. Soon, media products will begin to mirror the public's heightened level of psychological functioning. Themes reflecting uplifting List A qualities of the heart and spirit will become more commonplace. In the not too distant future, people will look back on the typical media products of today as one symptom of the lower quality tastes and preferences of a culture that had innocently lost touch with the natural source of high quality mental functioning.

Organizations and Businesses

In trying to create more effective and productive business organizations, managers, supervisors, and personnel directors alike have used a variety of traditional psychological models. Borrowing from these models, they have formulated hundreds of tools and techniques to improve organizational problem-solving, communication skills, decision-making, stress management, group dynamics, motivation, and productivity. None of these techniques, however, has led to long-term resolutions of serious organizational problems such as high absenteeism, stress, substance abuse, work-related injuries, low productivity, conflict, poor morale, theft, and workplace violence. Why? Because the true source of lasting change is not to be found in tools or techniques. The only true source of enduring organizational change is the rekindling of employees' inherent healthy psychological functioning.

In any organization, conflicts between staff and management, among workers, and between departments are always the result of unrecognized processing mode thinking misuses and the insecure feelings they awaken. Roger Mills describes this condition as follows:

> "...Negativity is as detrimental to the smooth running of an organization as friction is to the smooth running of an engine. Managers who feel insecure and who do not know what this feeling means and how it is produced, will focus on some form of self-protection. They will be on the lookout for trouble. They will talk down to employees, have an elevated idea of their own importance, and guard this image of self-importance with their lives. They will be reluctant to admit mistakes and will tend to blame problems on someone or something else. They will not look to themselves to discover their role in the problem. They will overlook the fact that, as

organizational leaders, they have knowingly or unknowingly contributed to whatever situation exists."

When more people understand the principles of Psychology of Mind, there will be a transformation in how organizations function. Administrators, for example, will start to take more personal responsibility for their organizations. This responsibility will not be motivated by fear, guilt, or blame...it will arise instead from understanding, common sense, and wisdom. Managers will start treating their employees with more respect and compassion. They will look for ways to help them do their jobs more easily and efficiently.

Motivated out of clearer vision and higher-order feelings, management will more sensibly use the skills, talents, and resources of each employee. Managers will understand moods and how insecurity is produced. They will know how to guide employees to higher quality thinking where their feelings and perceptions will automatically change for the better. They will understand that when employees feel good they tend to do well. Thus, they will see the futility in trying to motivate people through fear and control. Instead, these enlightened managers will use more common sense, practical ways to support employees in accessing the natural, healthy motivation that comes from the stream.

With a shift in understanding, management will lead employees to new levels of cooperation, productivity, and work satisfaction. Soon the health of our organizations will leap forward, characterized by a heightened level of collegiality, creativity, and mutual respect. Productivity will burgeon, while stress, burnout, and other dysfunctional behaviors will diminish or disappear.

Psychodiagnostics and Psychotherapy

My sister, Kathy, is presently enrolled in an external degree program of a prominent college in the southeast. She is working on her Master of Arts degree in mental health counseling. One requirement for this degree is the completion of an on-campus week of psychological testing and group therapy. The purpose of this requirement is for the program faculty to assess the mental health of each prospective counselor.

As part of this assessment, each student was required to complete a psychological test called the MMPI. This test is the godfather of personality inventories in the field of psychology. The MMPI consists of about 540 questions. For each question the respondent answers "yes," or "no" depending on whether the item applies to him or her. A typical question would be something like, "I need the support of my friends and family in order to feel secure." A "no" response to this type of question, and a sub-group of several others like it, would be scored in the "pathological" direction. Put another way, if a respondent answers most of the questions of this type in a similar fashion, he or she would score low on the test sub-scale that measures "succorance," or dependency needs. This means that that individual would be viewed as being in denial of their supposed dependence upon or need for other people to feel secure, fulfilled, and worthwhile.

That's exactly what happened to my sister. Kathy is reasonably well-grounded in the principles of Psychology of Mind. She realizes that the experiences of security and well-being come from the inside-out, not from the outside-in. She clearly loves her friends and family. She prefers their support and approval, but doesn't experience it as the source of her well-being. Thus, she answered all of the "succorance" questions on the MMPI in a manner that landed her in the "pathological" category.

Following the testing, a faculty member from the program met with my sister to discuss her test results. At that meeting, Kathy tried to explain her MMPI "succorance" responses within the framework of the principles of Psychology of Mind. In other words, she tried to tell the faculty member that genuine experiences of security, autonomy, and well-being come from the inside-out. She explained that she deeply loved her family and friends, but that she didn't experience her worth or well-being as tied to them.

The faculty member, however, viewed my sister's test results, as well as her explanation, through the programmed thoughts of her theoretical orientation. Actively processing these biased thoughts, all this faculty member could see was that my sister must be "in denial!" With her natural intuition overwhelmed by the noise of indiscriminately processing her theoretical memories, this faculty member couldn't see what was so...the healthy state of mind of my sister, the person sitting in front of her!

At the conclusion of the interview, the staff member recommended that my sister enter psychotherapy to deal with "conflicts related to her succorance needs." By then, Kathy realized that she was being seen through some pretty low quality thinking. Thus, she quickly agreed to follow the counseling recommendation.

Startled by this spontaneous agreement, the faculty member responded, "You weren't supposed to say that...according to the test results, you're supposed to be in denial and should fight me about going into therapy." To this Kathy replied, "Well, I'm not going to fight with you and, if you think that counseling is needed, I'm willing to do it." Later, I told her that she might have said, "I'm not in denial...de Nile is de river in Egypt." Just kidding!

There's nothing wrong or ill-advised with developing and using psychological tests or inventories. However, the field has generally failed to understand that the majority of its current psychological inventories are derived from archaic theories of human behavior that anchor people to their problems, their pasts, their personality...emphasizing negativity and limitations. As a result, the tests formulated from these theories often box people in to the very realities that they're trying to escape. When the field understands the principles of Psychology of Mind, a more factual, accurate, and practical group of psychological tests will then be developed.

Furthermore, the field of psychotherapy has been operating within the limits of repeatedly processing its biased theoretical thoughts. At the present time, there are over 200 different theories or models of human psychological functioning recognized by the

American Psychological Association. Each of these approaches focuses mainly on psychological dysfunction or pathology. Each promotes a different approach to treatment and prevention. Each of these models and derivative therapeutic approaches is a product of the very functioning it seeks to explain. Each has innocently missed the essential recognition of the universal principles of psychological functioning; Mind, Consciousness, and Thought.

A breakthrough to an advanced psychology can not occur through processing the thoughts of any particular theory. Yet behind all of these theories is the principle of thought that was used to formulate each perspective. When the field understands the principles of Psychology of Mind, it will shift from confusion and diversity to clarity, simplicity, and power in its understanding of human psychological functioning. With a shift in understanding, theorists and practitioners alike will be empowered to break through the limits of the realities spawned by habitually processing of their biased theoretical memories. They will then discover practical, common sense approaches to empower people to understand their psychological functioning and access the natural, free-flowing source of their inherent mental health.

Education

When children chronically misuse their processing thinking, they come to school feeling insecure. Thus, their natural interest in learning and ability to process information objectively is contaminated. Their lower quality thinking habits result in high levels of self-consciousness, making it harder for them to concentrate, follow directions, and feel at ease in the classroom.

When a child's natural self-esteem is overridden by misusing Mode Two, he will experience urges to prove himself, perhaps by acting out in the school setting. To the extent that a child perceives his worth to be at stake in learning situations, he will tend to see learning as hard and aversive. Ultimately, this can lead to a negative, self-perpetuating spiral that can culminate in high levels of school failure, dropout, delinquency, and substance abuse.

When the educational field understands the principles of Psychology of Mind, there will be a dramatic shift in perspective for educational administrators, teachers, and students alike. Teachers will begin to see how their students' states of mind affect their ability to learn and function appropriately in school. They will notice how their own moods, as well as their reaction to their students' moods, can dramatically affect their ability to draw out the natural health and motivation in children. Through this shift in understanding, and the wisdom and creativity it unleashes, teachers will be empowered to create a more optimal motivational climate in the classroom.

Teachers and administrators will begin to recognize that student acting-out behavior is a signal that they are misusing Mode Two thinking, and have moved into less secure states of mind. Thus, they will avoid taking their students' insecure moods personally. They will be less likely to "trigger" or exacerbate their students' processing mode abuses. Instead, they will intuitively remain on their students' side, while being firm and consistent at the same time. Where it makes sense, they will incorporate the principles of Psychology of Mind into the curriculum. By so doing, they will begin to rekindle the original excitement and enthusiasm they once brought to their work.

Soon, the overall organizational climate of our schools will be transformed into a warm, attractive, and engaging environment. Schools will begin to function efficiently and with minimal stress. They will become professionally rewarding, enjoyable, and productive settings for all school staff. In time, it will be typical for students and teachers to work together in cooperative and joyful learning experiences. Student learning and achievement will spiral upward, motivated by insight, curiosity, and inspiration. Students and teachers alike, will look forward to school as a place for exhilarating accomplishment, mastery, and full self-expression.

Politics and Government

Winston Churchill once said, "You can always count on the American Congress to do the right thing after they've tried all the other possibilities." If there was ever an institution that operated within the vicious spiral of processing mode abuse, insecure feelings, and maladaptive behavior, it's the American political system. Today, when most people hear the word "politics," they automatically think of lies, manipulation, deceit, pay-offs, inconsistencies, negative campaigning, and gridlock. A recent survey found that the job that American parents would <u>least</u> like their children to have is that of President of the United States!

In our political system we have two major parties, the Republicans and the Democrats. It seems that these two camps are continually competing with each other about whose realities are the right ones. Within each major party are several sub-groups. Each of these factions tends to compete with the others for the advancement or triumph of one set of perceptions over the other. The end result of this misguided, processing mode generated, self-righteous inflexibility is that our country continues to go down many empty tunnels. Innocently, most of our politicians would rather "look good" or "be right" than handle the country's business in more sensible ways.

When politicians understand the principles of Psychology of Mind, there will be a vertical leap in the effectiveness of government. Republicans and Democrats alike will finally start listening to one another and to their constituents. They will begin to focus on the good and sensible aspects of their respective positions and political philosophies. They will start acting from their deep, underlying commitment to the well-being of people. They will begin moving the country forward toward prosperity in ways that are fair and include everyone.

With a shift in understanding, there will arise a spirit of cooperation in governing never before imagined. Legislation will become lean on pork, and fat on common sense. Obvious governmental waste will be eliminated, the budget finally balanced, the national debt eliminated, and the issue of poverty seriously addressed. Citizens will feel supported by their government in ways that will foster their natural desire to contribute and serve. Leaders will emphasize the healthy functioning and well-being of the people.   The country will come together through shared understandings that will unleash a new level of maturity, common sense, and wisdom. A powerful national compassion will emerge from which solutions to America's worst social problems will naturally unfold!

International Relations

When people around the world understand the principles of Psychology of Mind, it will become clear on an international level that this paradigm represents a universally accessible answer to world peace. People will see the fact that thought and thought alone determines reality...including the reality of a world at peace!

Gordan Trockman, M.D., is a psychiatrist with the Hawaii Counseling and Education Center and a faculty member with the Psychology of Mind Training Institute. I'd like to share with you his vision of world peace as it applies specifically to the perennial dispute between the Arabs and the Israelis. Gordan envisions it this way:

"Suppose the Arabs and Israelis decided to start fresh. Never mind that people in the Middle East have been killing each other for several thousand years...from this day on, the past is left behind. Not forgotten, just left behind.

Suppose they were finally able to recognize that their differences arise from different thoughts about what constitutes a correct lifestyle, the right cultural values, the right way of naming God, and giving thanks - all their fighting was over different perceptions of the world, which quite naturally stem from these different thoughts.

The Arabs and Israelis would finally give up drawing lines in the hot, sandy desert, forbidding one another to cross. They would be able to see how foolish it is to kill a man because he has different thoughts about the world...we all have different thoughts. No two people in the world have the same thoughts. This is a psychological fact of life, which once discovered and accepted, brings understanding and tolerance for others with other thoughts, other world views.

The actual feeling of peace comes via thought, as does a feeling of anger. Whatever is on a person's mind at a given moment creates their feelings at that moment. Peace is only a thought away...it depends on letting go of negative thoughts, memories, and beliefs from the past. After all, such thoughts and memories are only as important as the person thinking about them thinks they are.

Imagine two teams, the Arabs and Israelis: from the higher elevations, they could bring water down to irrigate the desert. They could hold a competition to see which team grows the most food. The team that won would have the honor of giving the festival at the end of the season. At first, these high-spirited teams might look at the other team working and make fun, perhaps laughing about the way the others dress. 'Look at those long robes, they are really setting themselves back with all that clothing.' Then they would notice, 'Oh, they can work a half hour longer in the sun than we can because they dress like that...maybe we should try it, or they are going to win the contest.'

They would start to learn from each other. They would see that with co-operation, all can co-exist in peace. All their energy would go into constructive activities. No more energy wasted on negativity and violence. At the end of the season, they would probably have food left over, which could be sent to hungry children somewhere else in the world.

All it would take for this to happen is for a sufficient number of people in the region to realize how thought works. Thought creates our reality from within our own minds. People create their perception of the world from their thinking, then step out into the world to play the game of life according to the way they see it...they don't see a single 'reality,' they see 'a reality.' A man or woman always has the ability to change his or her mind. A small change, but a giant leap for the evolution of the human race."

The value to individuals, families, organizations, even countries, in understanding the principles of Psychology of Mind is incalculable. As more and more people understand, the vision of a world that works for everyone will be transformed into a reality whose time has come. You are now positioned to make a profound contribution to this future. You are already making a huge difference. Living from your new level of understanding, you are automatically designing this future now!

HOW GOOD CAN YOU STAND IT!

Making a Difference

T he end of our journey is at hand. It's been a privilege for me to serve as your coach. Thank you for letting me contribute to you by sharing the transformational principles of Psychology of Mind. Thank you for being coachable.

Whether you realize it or not, you have been my coach as well. I've moved to a new level of understanding during our journey together. Thank you for <u>your</u> coaching. Thank you for <u>your</u> contribution. Thank you for <u>your</u> vision!

Another natural by-product of experiencing a breakthrough in understanding is the desire to make a difference in the lives of other people. When people experience a powerful shift in perspective, they naturally want to share it with others. We've experienced the profound difference that the principles of Psychology of Mind can make in people's lives. We've envisioned a world that will start working for everyone as more people understand. When people break through to a new level of awareness, they automatically experience a desire to contribute to people...a natural inclination to share the new possibilities they see with others.

With your permission, I'd like to offer one last bit of coaching about contribution and service. Perhaps the best way to contribute to other people is by staying in the stream and trusting your free-flowing thinking to show you the way. Thinking primarily in the free-flowing mode and simply being with people is a gift all by itself. Living in the intelligent stream of responsive, gliding thought will naturally reveal to you other ways to contribute...ways that are wise and compassionate. I guarantee that whatever form your contribution takes, it will be a fulfilling and satisfying experience.

From the stream, your life will show up as a remarkable gift and you'll savor each precious moment. You will deeply appreciate life's simple things like the scent of lilacs in the spring, the smell of burning leaves on a crisp fall day, the touch of a friend's hand on your shoulder, an ice cream cone, a gentle breeze, a kiss on the cheek from a small child. The more you learn to trust and ease into free-flowing thinking, the more your experience of effortless happiness and inner peace will become a way of life. How good can you stand it? Please don't worry...from your new level of understanding...

YOU'LL STAND IT AS GOOD AS IT GETS!

Personal Coaching and Additional POM Resources

Additional Copies of *Falling In Love With Life:*

Additional copies of *Falling In Love With Life* can be ordered directly from Breakthrough Press. Volume discounts available. Call 1-800-920-8533 or use order form on next page.

Personal or Group POM Coaching with Dr. Tom Kelley:

Thomas M. Kelley, Ph.D.
600 N. Old Woodward, Suite 303
Birmingham, MI   48009

248-644-4909

Psychology of Mind Resource Center:

Additional POM books and tapes including *Falling In Love With Life* can be ordered directly through the Psychology of Mind Resource Center.

USA Office: Psychology of Mind Resource Center
2436 NW Torsway
Bend, OR   97701

1-800-481-7639

e-mail allan@pom-resource-center.com

Web Site www.pom-resource-center.com

Australian
Office:

7 The Avenue
Midland, Western Australia 6056

08-9274-8877

e-mail john@pom-resource-centre.com.au

Web Site www.pom-resource-centre.com.au

Order Form

Telephone Orders - Call Toll Free 1-800-920-8533

Please have your Master Card or Visa ready
100% Money Back Guarantee if not Thrilled!

Postal Orders -

    Breakthrough Press
    P. O. Box 81226
    Rochester, MI 48308-81226

Price - $19.95 US each

Sales Tax - Michigan Residents add 6% Sales Tax

Shipping - $3.95 US for the first book, $2.00 each
        additional book

Ship To:

Name: _____

Address: _____

City: _____ **State:** _____

Zip: _____

Payment: Total $23.90 or $25.10 for Michigan Residents

☐ Check

☐ Credit Card: ☐ Visa   ☐ Master Card

Card Number: _____

Name on card: _____

Exp. date: _____ / _____

Order Form

Telephone Orders - Call Toll Free 1-800-920-8533

Please have your Master Card or Visa ready
100% Money Back Guarantee if not Thrilled!

Postal Orders -

> Breakthrough Press
> P. O. Box 81226
> Rochester, MI 48308-81226

Price - $19.95 US each

Sales Tax - Michigan Residents add 6% Sales Tax

Shipping - $3.95 US for the first book $2.00 each
                additional book

Ship To:

Name: _____

Address: _____

City: _____ **State:** _____

Zip: _____

Payment: Total $23.90 or $25.10 for Michigan Residents

☐ **Check**

☐ **Credit Card:** ☐ **Visa**   ☐ **Master Card**

Card Number: _____

Name on card: _____

Exp. date: _____/_____